TO MARK AND SEAN

Squirrel on my Shoulder

Squirrel on my Shoulder

John Paling

British Broadcasting Corporation

Published by the
British Broadcasting Corporation
35 Marylebone High Street
London W I M 4 A A

I S B N 0 563 17639 3

First published 1979
© John Paling 1979

All photographs unless
otherwise credited
© Oxford Scientific Films 1979

Printed in England by
Balding + Mansell
Wisbech, Cambs.

Contents

Author's Acknowledgements

During this project, I have received assistance from too many people to mention them all individually. However, special thanks are due to Sally Foy and Philip Sharpe who helped Sammy through his early days and Monica Shorten and Alberto Vizoso for their valuable advice and interest throughout all our adventures with squirrels.

In addition, I gratefully acknowledge the co-operation and kindness of expert countrymen Den Wood and Alan Hartley, various officials of the Ministry of Agriculture, and the keepers and staff of Blenheim Palace Estate.

I am indebted to all our friends and ex-colleagues of the Department of Zoology, Oxford, for all their patient assistance, information and good will. In fairness, I must make clear that any errors in the book are my own responsibility and have occurred unintentionally despite the guidance of my more academic colleagues.

I also thank Victoria Huxley and Charles Elton of BBC Publications for their considerable contributions in the roles of editor and designer for the book and David Thompson and George Bernard for help in chronicling Sammy's life on film and in stills.

Finally, I warmly thank my fellow directors of Oxford Scientific Films for sharing with me more than a decade of good companionship and immense enjoyment – Gerald and David Thompson, Peter Parks, Sean Morris, Ian Moar and John Cooke.

John Paling Oxford, 1979

Part One

1 Sammy's Home

This is a story about probably the most famous grey squirrel in the world. He was nicknamed Sammy and was the star of a BBC natural history film for the Wildlife on One series which is seen by an estimated ten million people in Britain and millions more in Europe and America.

It is also a story about one well-intentioned wildlife photographer who was nearly driven to tear his hair out because of the chaos and upsets that Sammy brought to his domestic life. I am a founder-director of Oxford Scientific Films, a company formed by a group of ex-Oxford University biologists some ten years ago to produce wildlife documentaries for television. Over that time, we have filmed hundreds of animals across the world, yet Sammy was the only one who has ever occupied such a special place in my heart. He came out of the blue from a friend who knew I was to make a film on squirrels, and he stayed to take over my life.

The first grey squirrels came to Britain from North America just over one hundred years ago; in 1876 four squirrels, probably the first four to arrive, were released at Henbury Park in

Cheshire and subsequently increased and spread. They seemed so lovely and appealing to the British that more and more were captured in America and brought over to at least thirty different places in Britain for display and release in zoos, country estates and city parks. They were welcomed with delight by the public who viewed them at that time as ornamental exotics.

Today, of course, they have spread throughout the country and their population is now so great that not even experts will guess at their total numbers. In contrast, the red squirrel has been long established in Britain but it had never been very abundant in most of the country and as the grey squirrels spread, the reds became less conspicuous. This fact, together with the damage to trees that the grey squirrels were causing, led to a mood of increasing unpopularity for the greys. Within fifty years of their first arriving here, it was realised that grey squirrels were getting out of hand and there was a total reversal of attitude towards them as the Government set out to try to slaughter every grey squirrel on British soil. A law passed in 1932 and still in operation today makes it illegal for the public to keep squirrels, to provide shelter for them, to entice them into gardens or even to feed them. They were outlawed and for many years the authorities operated a scheme of putting a price on the head (or more accurately the tail) of every grey squirrel that was killed.

They were branded as 'tree rats'; they were said to take the eggs and young of garden birds; they were seen to eat the gardener's crops and flower bulbs and increasingly there were claims that they were eating red squirrels and doing immense damage to British woodlands.

Yet, as will be seen, we now know that many of the 'facts' that surround the life history of the grey squirrel are not strictly accurate. That was why it was such a fascinating challenge to try to put the record straight and to record on film the truth about the grey squirrel in Britain. There seemed no better way than to follow the life of one particular animal – Sammy – as a

representative of all his kind. However, because of circumstances we could never have foreseen, the story was to develop
an unexpected, yet fascinating new dimension.

In preparation I read all the books about squirrels that I could
find and consulted specialists studying the animals in universities
and government departments. Using all this information, I
drafted an outline for the programme. Unfortunately, we were
never able to talk to the squirrels in advance for, when the time
came to do the filming, it became clear that they had not read the
script! They showed an almost total lack of co-operation in
carrying out normal squirrel behaviour as predicted by the
experts.

But one prediction remained frustratingly true. Even before I
started everyone agreed that the most difficult sequences to film
would be the intimate breeding sequences which mainly take
place in winter when the animals are holed up in their leafy nests
or dreys.

Here is an opportunity to lay to rest one common myth about
the grey squirrel in Britain: they do not hibernate in the winter.
In fact most of them mate in January and then the babies arrive in
late February, March and April in those balls of leaves and grass
that are so conspicuous in the stark winter trees. Not all dreys
hold mothers and young of course, and not all dreys are visible in
the open branches. The most secure squirrels are those born in
identically constructed dreys inside hollow trees, particularly
oaks. There are few old oaks that do not have some suitable holes
for squirrels as a result of branches breaking off and the effects of
winter weather rotting a still living tree.

Near to the studios of Oxford Scientific Films there is an ideal
site for grey squirrels – the extensive parkland of Blenheim
Palace. Though the palace, started in 1704, is venerated as
historic it is as nothing compared to some of the trees that are still
thriving in the grounds. The whole area was part of the ancient
primeval Wychwood Forest which was a royal possession well

before the Domesday Book and was used for hunting deer and wild boar by most of the early kings of England.

Many of the oak trees that were already mature when Henry VIII or Charles I passed through are still standing – gnarled, massive, contorted, split and almost invariably hollowed. Walk through the park today and there is a fair chance you may disturb a squirrel which will run up a tree and disappear somewhere inside. That squirrel could well be Sammy for he started life in front of the peeping eye of the camera lens in one of those very trees. The only difference was that, before all this happened, one of those giant oaks – estimated at between six hundred and a thousand years old – was transported and replanted outside my office window for the specific purpose of it serving as a grey squirrel maternity ward!

Our experts were unanimous in advising that we would be very lucky to get squirrels to give birth or to feed their young in front of the cameras and that our only real chance was to keep a population of wild squirrels captive and provide them with a suitable hollow oak so big that we could get inside the tree with our cameras and lights in advance of the animals using it as their boudoir.

It took about three months and £1000 to select a suitable old oak, obtain the necessary permissions to move it and then recreate a part of the woodland environment in a 30′ × 25′ × 20′ enclosure in the grounds of Oxford Scientific Films.

Naturally one would not think of chopping down a live venerable oak that may well have started its days around 1066. Instead the search was for a tree that was now dead but still standing, one whose days were numbered because of the estate's concern to ensure that none of these ancient trees were a danger to public safety. Of all the trees in the park, only one lone majestic oak seemed ideal for our squirrels. It stood about sixty feet high and was completely dead. Starlings had made their nests in some of the holes and it was possible to climb right up inside it. This was the tree that we pinned our hopes on.

It is to the credit of the land agent of Blenheim that he even considered my impertinent request to take the tree. He was all too aware of the damage that squirrels do to forestry plantations – including his own – and he unambiguously hated them. What chance that he would support my request to the Duke of Marlborough to saw through the twelve-foot-diameter base of that old oak and transport it the one and a half miles to our studios? All for the sake of providing grey squirrels with somewhere to breed! As he pointed out, it would almost have been simpler to build a vast enclosure around the tree rather than try to fell such a monster intact.

Yet word finally came back that we could have the tree. Although we didn't yet have our baby squirrel, we did have its home.

For several days I went into the palace grounds and surveyed the giant tree like a diamond cutter appraising his raw stone. Where should the tree be cut to get the best section with the most suitable holes for squirrels to use as a home? The enormity of the task began to dawn on me as I realised that by sawing the tree in half I would effectively get two massive oaks to transplant to my studio enclosure. The top section of the original tree alone would have a base diameter of about six feet – much larger than the biggest oak most people have seen. So we decided to make two squirrel trees from the one we had chosen. Now the woodsmen could get to work.

It took seven men to bring down the tree. Although one skilled operator could have felled the tree in a few minutes with a modern chain saw, we needed the massive tree to be lowered gently to the ground so that the main branches did not break and the bark did not shatter when the tree crashed down. This required three heavy mobile cranes to tie their metal hawsers to the top of the tree and to try to pull against its weight as it began to fall. The whole of the tree was wrapped in a cocoon of old carpets and sacking so the bark would not shake from the tree at the moment of impact.

The howl of the saw began at the base of the old giant. The machines, engines roaring, took up the tension on their hawsers as the tree began to sway. Little by little the saw separated the massive trunk from the soil that had supported it for countless centuries.

Gradually the cranes took over, the tree swayed, spun a little on its base, then with a deafening accompaniment of diesel engines it fell to the ground dragging two of the cranes along with it. There was a crash of branches, the tree bounced back away from the ground before settling in a flurry of dust and broken branches. We rushed to the spot to find that luck was with us and, for our purposes, the squirrel's home was essentially undamaged.

With the noise still ringing in our ears, and the girth of the fallen tree extending above us nearly twice our height, the huge proportions of the old oak were awesome. However a sense of human perspectives was brought to the scene by the arrival of a dapper man walking a tiny, fluffy dog on a tartan lead. He had watched the operation from a distance and began, 'Excuse me please, but I wonder if you'd mind, perhaps . . . would it be possible for me to have some of the teeny bits of bark for my flower arrangement classes?' No one could answer with a straight face.

The next job was to saw the tree in half and transport each part to the grounds of our film studios where they were stood upright once again by a twenty-one-ton crane. Each half looked exactly like an old tree in winter and very soon when the vegetation had grown around them, it seemed as if they had actually grown there.

Now we had the basis of Sammy's home. The trees were so big and hollow we could get inside them by sawing a door in the back and then hopefully film the squirrels' private life within.

The idea was that a female squirrel was to give birth in the tree and the life of one of her babies would be followed through the film. We had already nicknamed it 'Sammy' immaterial of its sex.

As every expert on wildlife knows, it is important to keep animals in conditions as close to their natural environment as possible. So it was that we planted around our oak trees several trees that we knew grey squirrels liked. A typical grey squirrel habitat in Britain is a mixed woodland (with a high proportion of oak trees) and so we planted more oak trees, this time living ones, together with sycamore, beech and maples. Some under-growth plants and bracken were added and then Ian Hendry, OSF's construction expert undertook the massive task of erecting the frame and netting to complete the huge enclosure.

So Sammy's birthplace was made ready. But our problems had just begun.

2 Sammy's Mum

Once the big problem of a suitable home was settled, it was a simple matter to capture a female and a male squirrel and then let nature take its course. At least, that's what we thought! But we had not taken account of the fact that, although grey squirrels breed all too successfully in the wild, in captivity they exercise the most rigorous form of family planning. In fact hardly anyone in the world has ever persuaded captive animals to mate although their basic breeding cycle is well known.

In late December and January, courtship normally takes place. Several males may chase after a single female high in the trees causing quite a commotion, seemingly oblivious to any onlookers. The males make a low chattering noise and threaten each other for the right to mate with the female. The whole procedure is accompanied by much flicking and circling of the tail by the male and occasional screams from the female whose behaviour often suggests a marked reluctance to co-operate. During February the females are usually pregnant and spend an increasing time adding to their dreys and then driving away all other animals and spending more and more time in their nests. Development inside the mother takes about forty-five days and the babies are born weighing around half an ounce each (1.7 grams). Three is the average litter size and each baby is initially pink, blind and relatively helpless.

They are fed on their mother's milk for about ten weeks and start emerging from their dreys from the end of April onwards up to May and June. While most animals breed in the winter, some have a second breeding season which begins in June, producing babies mainly in August, and the young begin to leave the nests at the end of September. All this relates to squirrels in the wild. In captivity they have similar breeding seasons, if they breed at all. All we could do as newcomers was to take the advice of those few experts who *had* managed to arrange the necessary conditions for squirrels to mate successfully. Although no one felt sure about what the essential ingredients were, it seemed that several factors had to be taken into consideration in order to give ourselves the best chance of being the first people to record the early life of a family of grey squirrels.

First the enclosure needs to be large so that the male can chase the female around as part of his courtship. Too small a cage, it was thought, might deprive the pair of squirrels of enough space for them to play their form of hide and seek and follow-my-leader which seems a necessary preliminary to successful mating.

In this instance, we felt we had given our animals more than enough space with a purpose-built landscape garden which had been specifically directed at what we understood were squirrel preferences.

Secondly, the enclosure needed to be quiet and undisturbed. By arranging our enclosure to be outside one end of our studios set in the wooded countryside eight miles from Oxford, we felt encouraged that we could probably offer as good a spot as any.

Next came the crucial question of the choice of animals, the number to keep and the balance of the sexes. On this, our advisers were fairly precise. Given the size of our enclosure and all the available nesting spaces, we were recommended to have seven adults, two males and five females. It was predicted that the males would dominate and that some competition for mates on the part of the males might help the development of a situation whereby both animals were eager to mate, to become Sammy's father in fact.

The scientists had one more recommendation to help our chances but this was more difficult to fulfil. 'If possible,' we were told, 'get animals of at least two years of age.' As squirrels are all adult within a year of birth, and there is no easy way of ageing them, this meant that any we caught from the wild might be below this recommended maturity.

In the wild, the average age of a grey squirrel is only one and a third years. They will live much longer than that – up to twelve years in fact – but it remains true that most squirrels probably only pass through one breeding season before they die. However older animals that have already gone through one or more breeding seasons were considered to be the best bet for our chosen parents on the basis that there is no substitute for experience.

Hence a call went out along the squirrel experts' grapevine for any animals of at least two years of age that might be available for my breeding programme. By good fortune it turned out that our friends in the zoology department at Oxford University had a few they had been keeping under observation for over a year and so we started out with those. Two more individuals also arrived having been brought up by people who found them as squirrel orphans after their parents had been killed in a previous year. Once we had obtained the necessary government licences, five potential mothers and two mature and, hopefully, virile males were imported into our enclosure and we waited to let nature take its course while we prepared ourselves to observe the courtship ritual of the animals.

We waited eagerly for this to begin once our squirrels had

settled down and December 1977 had arrived. Sadly there was no sign whatsoever of any courtship behaviour. As January and February passed by, it became clear that something was seriously wrong. None of our carefully selected potential parents had followed the text books. Sammy Squirrel, the star, and hero of our film, had not been born. To make matters worse, we were also filming wild squirrels out in the woods around Oxford and they too showed no sign of being aware that the main breeding season for adult squirrels in Britain starts with mating in December and January. We appeared to have chosen the very winter to make our film when the squirrels of Oxford simply didn't breed!

In an effort to find out more about the breeding season, we went out with gamekeepers on their squirrel shoots in the winter and early spring to see if any baby squirrels were being found. The keepers work hard to keep down the squirrel population levels on their estates by pushing out the leafy dreys with long poles and firing at the animals as they flee. Sometimes dislodged dreys contain babies which fall to the ground unharmed, cushioned by the ball of vegetation.

But to no avail. It simply confirmed that no local squirrels were breeding that year. What's more, enquiries from scientists and countrymen from all over England revealed that, apart from a few isolated pockets, it was a nationwide phenomenon. The books on squirrels had never bothered to tell us and only later did we learn that, on occasions, the animals *will* skip a whole breeding season if conditions are unsuitable.

Looking back to the previous autumn of 1977 there had been an almost total lack of acorns and beech nuts and this may well have affected the condition of the overwintering squirrels and put them off mating. To explain why there should have been so few nuts that particular year, it is probably necessary to go further back. 1976 had been one of the driest years on record throughout Britain and the trees had responded by delivering a

staggeringly heavy nut crop. 1975 was also good for nut pro-
duction and these two years together appear to have exhausted
the trees' capacity for bearing fruit for the very year when I took
an interest. Whatever the reasons, very few squirrels bred in the
winter of 1977 and I was left with a film without a film star.

So as the season moved on, I made efforts to encourage our
animals to breed during the summer months when, in the wild,
some grey squirrels are reported to breed again. Not knowing
what else we could do, we increased their food supply,
supplementing their diet with a wide variety of natural foods.
We waited and watched but in the end we had to accept that
they were still not interested.

By now, however, we had fallen back on a second alternative
which was to capture a wild female squirrel that was already
pregnant. We reasoned that if we made such an animal at home
in a new, specially constructed and isolated breeding enclosure,
we stood a good chance of being on hand to record the birth of
the litter and to film their upbringing by the mother. We
obtained special traps constructed to capture live squirrels and
we set them during July in the woodlands around Oxford. We
caught a few females and received others from scientists
studying the animals miles away in the south of England. In a
typical year, about half of these would be expected to be
pregnant and so we tried to determine for ourselves whether any
of them actually were. One way of investigating this is to
transfer the squirrels from the traps into a simple wire netting
tube constricted and closed at one end, and then to probe gently
with one's fingers over their belly to see if developing babies can
be detected. However when we did this, once again we could
not make a definite diagnosis. Even if there were baby squirrels
within, their weight might be masked by the amount of food
that the animals would consume at any one time. A new
approach was necessary.

The idea came to me on the London Underground when I

spied an advertisement offering a confidential service of pregnancy testing – no questions asked. What would they diagnose, I wondered, from urine samples from a few of my squirrels? Returning to Oxford I set out to obtain samples from each of my potential mothers but found the task far harder than I had imagined. The first difficulty was that the squirrels had to be captured and moved to a convenient holding enclosure. However, they invariably became excited at the halfway stage while being transferred in a darkened sack bag and in their panic they released the contents of their bladders into the sacking. Experience soon showed that it was not possible to wring a sample out from that. We didn't do much better even with those animals we kept in separate cages with a netting base, below which was a collecting tray. Their sample was typically made up of half spilt drinking water, a few droppings and various peanut shells and fragments of bedding. As it was proving so tricky, I took the precaution of 'phoning a friend in the pregnancy testing service of a local hospital to ask her opinion as to whether it was worth continuing. She felt very doubtful if the techniques applied to humans would work. Unless I could provide samples from a known pregnant as well as a non-pregnant female, she felt that it would not be possible to make a valid diagnosis. 'However, if you want to bring in four or five samples for us to test,' she continued, 'we'll give it a try.' At this stage the very idea of me, a man, walking through a pregnancy clinic crowded with expectant ladies and bearing, not one, but four tubes containing different samples was just too much for my reputation! There must be another way.

Once in touch with the medical world, the next obvious technique to try was X-rays. Although this technique had apparently not previously been used for squirrels, we received the generous advice and co-operation of the Department of Radiology of the University of Oxford. We were assured that by using small doses and modern techniques of recording, there was a negligible chance that any possible babies inside the squirrels might be harmed. So we put our four most likely candidates into separate cages and set out for the local medical centre. We covered the cages with rugs and coats so the animals would not be frightened in transit and also to avoid shocking any human patients we might have encountered. Once inside, it didn't take long to improvise a transparent tube to restrain them while X-ray pictures were taken of their abdomens. Four handfuls of fur and the odd bite later, we had the news we had been waiting for. None of them showed signs of pregnancy. Two weeks later, another four patients had appointments made for them and once again the X-ray beams were directed towards unusual short plastic tubes with a bushy tail protruding from each one. Again all negative. We kept some of the animals and none of them subsequently showed signs of pregnancy.

The conclusion was inescapable. For the second possible breeding season, we had failed to persuade any female to give birth and so provide us with even a single picture of the central character which was to start our programme.

3 The Arrival of Sammy Squirrel

Although we had discovered that no squirrels were being born in our area during the winter breeding season of 1977, we learnt that a few had in fact bred elsewhere. Foresters and gamekeepers had been carrying out their regular policy of shooting adult squirrels in winter from dislodged dreys. It was from such a source that my friend Dr Alberto Vizoso first obtained Sammy.

As part of his research into the viruses of squirrels Dr Vizoso had accompanied a shooting party into one of the areas where babies had been reported and by the end of the day, 8 April 1978, he brought back alive seven baby squirrels. None of them had their eyes open. They were pink and helpless. They were all from different litters and so of different ages. The mothers had all been shot, or had had to desert them while escaping. There was no squirrel's milk for them to feed upon and they desperately needed warmth and attention. Knowing of my interest in squirrels, he kindly 'phoned me and asked if I wanted to have a go at keeping them alive. It would be very difficult to keep them healthy, he explained, and they would demand a great deal of our time if they were to survive. As my family life revolved around squirrels for the duration of the film, there was no hesitation in accepting his offer and taking up the challenge. My children, Mark and Sean, jumped into the car with me and we were soon at Alberto's home where we met his wife, Monica Shorten, a squirrel expert in her own right. But the immediate centre of attraction was the shoe box which was the temporary home of the orphans. We peered into it and removed the top layer of cotton wool to the accompaniment of amazingly loud alarm calls and we were confronted with the flailing legs of freshly disturbed baby squirrels, all a vivid pink colour. The necks of the smallest were scarcely strong enough to hold their heads up and the dark eye bulges and the huge feet were their most conspicuous features.

Our hosts estimated that the three smallest babies of about two inches in length were only about five days old. Then there were others increasing in size, till the oldest would possibly be three weeks, still blind with effectively no fur, yet with large feet and claws extending from their fragile, scraggy bodies.

'The trick in keeping squirrels', we were told, 'is mainly to keep them warm, and then, secondly, to make sure they have the right amount of food – they will need something like six feeds a day over the whole twenty-four hours!'

We were loaded up with supplies of pipettes, some glucose to add to the squirrels' food for extra energy and much advice on their own experiences of looking after orphaned baby squirrels. Back home, the marathon began. We transferred the arrivals to a clean wooden box and kept them cradled in cotton wool on one edge of the top of the central heating system. When they were settled, we judged that the first feed should begin.

There are various ways that you can try to feed a baby squirrel but we were recommended to try to get them to feed on cow's milk. This requires special pipettes, little glass tubes with a squeezable rubber bulb at one end. The other end must be narrow and smooth so that it won't damage the young squirrels' mouths. The procedure to be followed was this: milk was sucked up into a glass pipette, and the nozzle was gently introduced between the toothless jaws of the tiny squirrels as they are held in the palm of a hand. Then milk was squirted gently into the mouth, and hopefully down the throat.

The operation was not as easy as it seems. For a start, the squirrels are by no means accustomed to having rounded glass tubes put into their mouths. The surface must be very unlike the pliable nipple of the mother they had so recently been feeding from. What happened usually was that the milk went in the mouth and then squirted out through the side; or the squirrel turned its head away so that the milk squirted all over its nose, its eyes, and its body. But by and large, with a bit of effort, we managed to squirt enough milk down in order to give them the energy to stay alive.

So for every four hours, day and night, each of the squirrels had to be fed on cow's milk. The procedure was really very tiresome, because in the first place we had to boil a kettle of water, sterilise the pipettes, and then warm the milk to a temperature which seemed comfortably around squirrel blood heat, then carry out the feed. Then, as it is often a messy job, more of the milk goes over the body of the animal than into the mouth. Despite these problems, and with the perseverance of the handler and the animal together, most of the squirrels, towards the end, got used to being fed this way, and came to suck eagerly upon the pipette.

It is also very important to clean the squirrels completely of any surplus milk. The reason for this is that milk is a very rich source of all sorts of nutrients and this is an ideal ground for bacteria to breed upon. Now, if the squirrels were to get it over their bodies, then bacteria and other diseases would begin to spread and could quite quickly cause their death. So in sequence the little squirrels had first of all to be fed, then bathed as thoroughly and gently as possible with warm water and cotton wool, and then dried in a soft towel, before being returned to their box. So one after the other was fed, washed, dried and put back, until quite commonly the whole operation took two hours from the start to finish leaving only a two-hour rest period before starting the whole lot again. Fortunately at this time, Sally, a friend of mine, helped me in the evenings to look after these animals, and we used to take it in shifts, one doing the feeding, one doing the cleaning and drying, and this halved the time that it took.

One weary evening – 12 April to be exact – she asked why cow's milk was chosen as the best substitute for natural squirrel's milk. 'Had this', she asked, 'been found to be the nearest milk type to a mother squirrel's own milk?' I remember that the answer produced a gleam in my eye the moment I said it.

'I think we're using cow's milk simply because it's so easy to get hold of. It's possibly not very similar to squirrel's milk and, if only we knew it, it's quite likely that some other species of animal produces milk that would be far more suitable for squirrels. In fact Monica Shorten once mentioned that she had heard it rumoured that someone had found that cat's milk is fairly similar to squirrel's.'

No sooner had this thought come into my mind than I wondered if by chance we could persuade a cat with kittens to mother some or all of these baby squirrels for us. This was particularly poignant because that night for the first time, digging deep into the cotton wool lining of the wooden box in which the babies were being kept, my hand clasped a moist, cold body of one of the squirrels. This was the first of the fatalities that we were to experience despite our best endeavours to provide them with all that they needed.

So this decided me. We made some enquiries at the local cat's home, an old country house run by Mrs Gray, who is so charming, kind and sentimental over animals that her hospitable family is literally overrun by eighty or so creatures. A 'phone call produced the response that there was, in fact, one single mother with three kittens that had only recently been taken in as a stray. As far as they knew this was the first time that this particular cat had given birth. She had a small litter and many more nipples than she would need in order to feed those three. So, with the lady's enthusiastic co-operation, we packed one of our squirrels into a separate snug box and set out on the sixteen or so miles journey to the cat's home, to see if we could persuade that particular cat to accept one of our squirrels into its family and to bring it up with her own kittens.

It was pure chance really which made us select the particular member of our six for the car journey. We didn't take one of the smallest for we felt they would be most vulnerable to any loss of heat or changes of temperature that our pilgrimage to the cat's home would involve. On the other hand, we didn't choose one of the larger ones for it seemed appropriate some-how that we used a middle-sized one for our test. It happened to be a male.

Our arrival at the cat's home was heralded surprisingly by the barking of dogs, for the good lady who ran it didn't only keep a whole menagerie of feline friends, but an assortment of canine ones too. Our knock at the door produced beaming faces and we were ushered in through a maze of lapping tongues and wag-ging tails to a room that was, to say the least, distinctive as a result of the long-time occupancy of the many cats. We were ushered through the first room into a corridor where there was a second battalion of other animals – more cats, more dogs and some hamsters – and upstairs to a bathroom where, locked in for security, were cats requiring special attention. In one corner, inside an enclosure containing a cardboard box, was a tortoise-shell-and-white cat. Her name, we were told, was Beauty.

Beauty didn't really seem at all concerned by our arrival. Our squirrel – who had by now assumed the name Sammy – was

safely out of sight in the warm cotton wool lining of a wooden
box, and its presence was obviously not detected. Beauty's three
kittens were initially hidden beneath her but she readily allowed
Mrs Gray to move her aside for us to glimpse her appealing
babies. She estimated they were five days old.

In Mrs Gray's opinion Beauty was as good and docile a
mother as she had ever experienced. If any cat was likely to be
tolerant of a stranger in the nest, she thought, it would be
Beauty. So the cage was moved aside, and we all made a fuss of
Beauty and her kittens. Beauty walked in rather a strange way,
having something of a limp, but because she was a stray and had
only arrived at the home three days before, Mrs Gray had no real
idea of what might have happened to her. However, the limp
certainly didn't affect Beauty's attention for her kittens. She also
had a little bit of a sniffle but this was easily overlooked by the
charming sight of the family. The three babies, eyes still closed,
sprawled after their mother as she was coaxed away from the
inside of the box. There was plenty of food and milk around for,
we were told, mother cats should always be given an excess of
both.

When Beauty had settled once more over her kittens, we decided to try out the crucial test that was the whole purpose of our
visit. I lifted Sammy from his cotton wool lining and, holding
him firmly in the palm of my hand so that virtually none of his
body could be seen, I began to stroke Beauty round the head
with the other hand. As I did so, I made sure that I covered her
eyes and turned her head away from her belly, while I carefully
pushed Sammy underneath the warm body to join the company
of the three little kittens. Continuing to stroke Beauty all the
while I moved my hand so that she could in fact see round down
her belly, though by now the young squirrel was safely tucked
away out of sight.

We paused and watched, our hands ready to dash in and grab
the squirrel back into safety if the cat should show any sign of

rejecting it or, even worse, snapping at it.

It seemed some time before Beauty realised that there was a stranger in the nest, for she carried on looking at us, and resting her head on her paws pensively. Down below, the baby kittens were suckling away and, we guessed, the squirrel was just lying low enjoying the warmth and contact. But in time the mother turned to lick some of the kittens, and as she did so her nose clearly picked out the scent of the stranger in the group, and, with our hands poised no more than inches from the squirrel, we watched in a tense silence as the mother cat started to lick the baby squirrel. She licked it hard and long, presumably in doing so, she transferred her scent on top of that of the squirrel. The other kittens paid no attention whatsoever to the newcomer, and after a while the mother cat settled down and ignored the outrageous new arrival. It was impossible for us to forget that the baby squirrel looked for all the world like a baby rat that the mother cat, in other circumstances, would snap up in a flash.

It was clear that the cat was not at all concerned by the newcomer in her nest. Her natural instincts were clearly to clean up her own kittens and she did the same for our visitor. It is my guess that if the kittens begin to smell of urine or faeces then it is that smell that first signifies to the mother that the babies are due for a clean-up. It seems likely that the alien smell of the squirrel produced the same response in Beauty.

Sammy, of course, didn't feed initially. He seemed happy just to snuggle down amidst his new stepbrothers or sisters, and after fifteen minutes we all agreed that there had not been the slightest sign that the cat was bothered by this new arrival, or even aware that her family had suddenly grown by one. So, with the agreement of all parties, Beauty and her kittens were put into a cat basket and the long journey back to my home in Bladon, Oxfordshire, had begun. Sammy during this time was transported once again in his separate box, for we did not wish to leave the squirrel with the cat and kittens during the journey.

As we said goodbye to Mrs Gray, she loaded us up with all we would need to keep the cat and kittens going for a day or two, and not only that but also there were fresh eggs from her chickens for our breakfasts. From now on, we were setting out on an adventure that was to give us even more sleepless nights!

4 The Invalids

When we finally arrived back home, the cat was released from the basket and explored the confines of my kitchen. It was again clear that she had a slight impediment in her walking for her back legs did not have the mobility one would normally expect · with a healthy cat. But she seemed happy enough, and certainly made a very faithful and dutiful mother. A smart wickerwork cat basket was lined with a photogenic blue rug and Beauty and her kittens were made to feel at home in their new surroundings. Our time away from the house had meant that the remainder of our infant squirrels were due for their cow's milk so we set about feeding them on the kitchen table where we could keep an eye on the cat family.

Almost immediately we uncovered the squirrels, we found another small, still, cold body in amidst the sprawling pink legs. This time, it was one of the middle-sized ones that had died. It began to seem all the more important to persevere with our unlikely scheme for using Beauty to help out in the rearing of our young dependants. Thus, before we started the marathon of feeding, washing and drying the remaining squirrels, we once again introduced Sammy under the belly of the mother cat, once again taking every precaution for fear that there should be any sign of antagonism from the mother. But, as before, Sammy wasted no time in burying himself deep down in the darkness and warmth underneath not only the cat, but also the kittens. We watched and waited, and once again the cat cleaned the squirrel together with her own babies. This led us to feel more satisfied that the impossible might just work. Could it really be that a cat, so naturally a hunter of things the size of a small mouse, might be persuaded to act as a foster mother for this one squirrel. We topped up the other four squirrels until their pink stomachs were almost white and balloon-like with milk. Finally, as Sammy did not feed from the mother cat, it was necessary to retrieve him for his late-evening dose of warmed cow's milk delivered in the usual manner.

It was late and we felt we had gone far enough that night and so we kept him separate from the cat family in case something should go wrong in our absence. The remainder of the squirrels showed no special reaction to Sammy as he snuggled down into the warm nest along with his kith and kin. Each animal seemed interested only in getting a position below all its nest-mates before a layer of cotton wool was loosely put on top to cover them.

As we wearily left our menagerie for the night, we talked of trying to foster several of the squirrels with Beauty on the grounds that she could probably cater for a bigger litter. However, we felt that to give her two or more infant squirrels could become something of a burden on the mother and so we resolved to limit our imposition upon her maternal care to one single squirrel.

We then reconsidered whether to start again and try to foster one of our smallest animals with Beauty but, looking ahead, we wanted to avoid having playful clawing kittens with a diminutive squirrel still in the nest. Equally it would not have been as

Right The dead oak tree in its natural setting in Blenheim Palace grounds

Below Building the squirrel set with the tree outside the studios

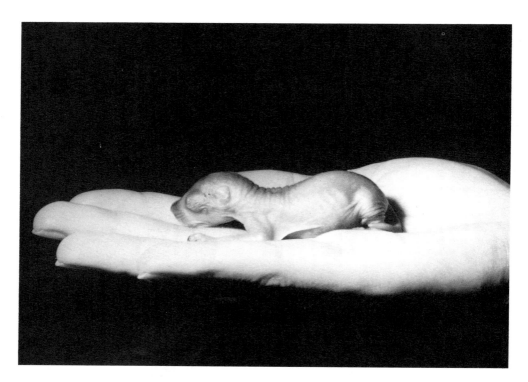

Above A young grey squirrel approximately 4 days old

Below A squirrel about $2\frac{1}{2}$ weeks old

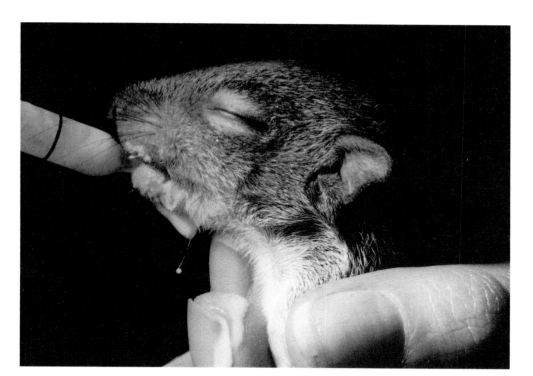

Above A squirrel being fed with a glass pipette at 3 weeks old

Below A squirrel at 5 weeks

Beauty suckling the three kittens and the orphan squirrel

Left Sammy at three weeks old

Below The mother cat licking milk from Sammy

One of the kittens 'play-
fighting' with Sammy.
On the right the kitten
adopts a typical fighting
posture by biting the
back of the squirrel's
neck

Sammy fighting back
against the kitten

interesting to have, say, a half-weaned squirrel hopping about while the kittens were relatively helpless and so, for this reason, we once again decided not to foster either of the older baby squirrels on the cat. So we came back to the same animal that had already been introduced to Beauty. He would be the one we would pin all our hopes on as he grew up as a member of Beauty's family. From then on, we labelled him 'Sammy Squitten'.

The next morning we stuck to our decision. Our much-travelled Sammy was again recovered from the nest of squirrels to be brought up under the care and attention of a foster mother, who, we hoped, had more to offer him than we did. It still seemed a long shot. The cat and kittens were as we had left them the night before, and this time as we transferred Sammy again, the squirrel was immediately welcomed by the cat. It would be wrong to say that Beauty recognised the squirrel, but she gave it her undivided attention, licking it hard all over as Sammy struggled to submerge himself out of sight. The mother showed no other reaction and it was difficult not to infer that she responded as if one of her kittens had been a temporary absentee from its nest. Once again the squirrel buried itself deep down below the litter and peace returned to the cat family.

Although one problem seemed to have been solved, at least for the present, there was still the fact that we had not managed to persuade Sammy to suckle and, if we did, whether the cat's milk would suit him. So now we moved to stage two.

As one of us stroked the cat, the other raised Sammy to a position opposite one of the pink nipples of the mother. The baby squirrel had been used to feeding on similar nipples back in his drey, but since then he had had to learn to suckle from the hard, inflexible glass tip of the feeding pipette. Now he was being given the chance to try again the warm sensation of a mother animal. However, Sammy Squitten seemed to have for-gotten everything he once knew about feeding from a mother.

Of course, the size of the nipples were much larger than those he would have been accustomed to on his real mother, but even though the mother cat was gently delivering milk, the squirrel could not be persuaded to hold his head over the source of all this goodness. At this time Sammy was only about three inches long, minus his tail. He had huge claws, disproportionately large for his size, and large, relatively rigid jaws. Already there were two large bottom teeth very clearly developed and quite pointed. To our eyes he looked very different from the bulky and fur-covered kittens that struggled to keep a grip on their mother. The situation began to look black but, after persevering for about twenty minutes, we managed to insert the nipple of the mother cat into the mouth of the little squirrel, and for a time he clung on, clearly responding instinctively to the mother's teat. However, he didn't seem to be making sucking movements with his throat, and after about half a minute he released his grip again.

Beauty during all of this time was being stroked and caressed as probably she had never been stroked before. Our aim was to divert her from the fiddling around that was taking place on her under surface. After a short rest, we tried Sammy once again on another nipple and although our fingers were being nuzzled by anxious kittens near at hand, this time we did manage to get Sammy to take the nipple and suddenly he jerked into action and started to suck eagerly upon it. Released from our grip, he simply lay against the mother's fur not holding on with hands or legs, but just clamped firmly to the nipple itself. From the movements of his throat and tiny belly it was quite clear that he was at last starting to feed. Sammy stayed there for a couple of minutes or so, pausing now and again, until he went into a state of rest. The kittens had all found a nipple for themselves at this stage. We stepped back from the mother cat as she adjusted her position to cover her kittens and their mess mate. For the moment, all seemed to be going well. There was no better place

Sammy could be, so we left him under the mother but kept a watchful eye on the situation while we attended to the remaining baby squirrels.

For the next few days, Sammy had to be initially encouraged each time before he would take a meal, but before too long we found him suckling all on his own amidst three much larger brothers and sisters, whose eyes, like Sammy's, were still not open to the strange bedfellow that would greet them. The mother cat during all of this time was docile and almost careless in the way she allowed us to handle her own babies as well as the pinkish, long-tailed, sharp-clawed alien. She seemed to show no difference in response towards our rodent at this stage. There was one obvious difference about Sammy in respect of his behaviour. Not only did he look totally unlike the other kittens, he also behaved unlike them. With his large claws, he was able to grip on to any rough surface. This is clearly a useful adaptation for a squirrel clinging on to the linings of the drey when the animal was in the wild, high in a wind-blown tree. But Sammy didn't only use his claws to hang on but also to preen himself or scratch with. There were times when, if the mother had left the basket to go and feed herself or to use the cat litter tray, the four babies would be left wallowing around in suddenly spacious and light surroundings. Then Sammy would frequently scratch himself rapidly all over as if preening himself down. In natural conditions, squirrel dreys are infested with many types of 'squatters' including fleas – so it is possible that the animals scratch to relieve some of the irritation caused by the insects as well as keeping their fur groomed and in good condition. On the other hand, it was evident that the kittens didn't need to preen themselves for the mother cat, with legendary thoroughness, would lick them vigorously with her rough tongue. This clearly had a cleansing action for their fur was left sleek and tidy after a thorough 'going over' by Beauty. It was conspicuous that Beauty gave far less attention to licking Sammy than she did to her kittens and this was the case for as long as we were able to keep our strange brood.

Ironically this difference in behaviour did not reflect a difference of parasitic 'hangers-on'. We soon became aware that Beauty and her babies were loaded with fleas! The usual evidence was there for all to see. The mother's neck and chest were particularly heavily infested and these were passed on to the kittens – and occasionally the odd one was seen scurrying over Sammy. The problem was made more urgent when we began to find that some of the fleas had hopped on to us. It takes an unusual sort of devotion to put up with a breeding colony of five hundred or so fleas in one's kitchen and to attend to the host animals every few hours.

For a moment the situation seemed to be only a temporary albeit distasteful setback for there are many brands of anti-flea powders on the market to choose from. All that seemed to be required was a trip to the chemists, a powder dusting over Beauty's fur and – bingo – all the fleas would vanish. But a second thought quickly dispelled that solution. How could we be sure that a chemical that would kill all the fleas would not kill Sammy Squitten? No pharmaceutical company would have tested their flea powder for the eventuality that an infant squirrel would be licking the fur of a cat covered in the powder. Presumably such powders didn't hurt cats or they couldn't be marketed but we didn't want to risk poisoning our perky orphan squirrel who at last seemed to be making good progress against already heavy odds. So for the time being, we lived with the fleas . . . and bathed a lot!

The feeding routine for the remaining squirrels continued as before. One evening, one of the smallest babies seemed weak and wouldn't swallow its milk. By next morning, that too was cold and stiff. Although this was the last thing we wanted, it so happened that with only three animals to feed by hand, I was spending less time with our brood and so stood the chance of catching up with some lost sleep. Sammy was now entrusted to Beauty full time and was feeding himself three days after his arrival. It was interesting to compare the amount of food that Sammy would take to that which the bottle-fed animals were being given. The hand-fed animals were allowed to drink as much cow's milk as they wanted and when they finished, their little bellies were so swollen they were almost like balloons. On the other hand Sammy stopped feeding when his little belly was hardly fat at all, yet obviously felt he had had sufficient food. This was further evidence for Dr Vizoso's earlier prediction that the quantity of food taken by a baby squirrel was less important than hygiene and essential warmth.

Only later did I learn that cat's milk is much richer and more nutritious than cow's milk. Apparently orphaned kittens cannot be maintained on cow's milk as they simply cannot take in enough volume to give them the nutrients they require. Another interesting sidelight was that for a long while Sammy seemed to take over a nipple all of his own. While the other members of the family, the kittens, would choose different nipples according to their taste or their location when the urge came upon them to feed, Sammy seemed to dominate the rear nearside nipple for about a week, before he occasionally ventured on to other nipples. What was very impressive was the strength of Sammy's limbs, especially his front legs and the claws on their long toes. For if any kitten attached itself to Sammy's personal nipple, he was quite capable of pushing in with great determination and usually he would displace the kitten and take up the nipple himself. For two or three days there was little more to report. It was clear that the cat had taken to Sammy and that the kittens effectively ignored him. Their concerns, like Sammy's, were for darkness and warmth and milk, all of which there were in abundance under the white belly of Beauty.

The mother cat not only cleaned up the wastes produced by

the kittens but obligingly she did the same for Sammy. On more than one occasion we observed that when Sammy 'spent a penny' he would crawl up and do so over one of the kittens at which point the mother would immediately lick her offspring clean. It is too much to suggest that because Sammy rarely was licked over himself, he developed that behaviour to get around a delicate personal problem!

Two days after their arrival, two of the kittens had their eyes open, and a day later the third joined them. It wasn't until two days later still that Sammy opened one eye and a day after that, the second. His strange world was just beginning to settle into a pattern and the little squirrel had become something of a local celebrity as various neighbours were let in on the secret. They came with wonderment in their faces to see what many must have thought to be an impossible sight: a mother cat placidly looking on as three kittens and a squirrel suckled from her, all with every air as if it was the most normal thing in the world.

But this idyllic scene was very short-lived for suddenly we found ourselves with a problem far more serious than the fleas. Beauty started to sneeze. After a while her eyes started to run, and to our grief it was clear she had developed cat 'flu. Beauty had a very bad bout of the disease and this resulted in her stopping eating, and during this time her supply of milk dried up. Her sneezes passed on the germs to the kittens, and two of the three also developed blocked up eyes and began to sneeze. We feared that any or all of them might die although Sammy showed no sign of having caught the disease. Just one of the immediate problems was that there was no food for anyone in the cat family. We reflected ruefully that, having got the cat to in part save us the problem of feeding one of our orphaned squirrels, at that stage we found ourselves with three baby squirrels still being hand-fed on cow's milk and now one mother cat, three kittens, and one 'squitten', also requiring nursing, hand-feeding and meticulous attention.

Naturally a visit to the local vet was called for, and not for the last time, the mother cat, the kittens and Sammy Squitten were put back into the travelling basket and transported by car to the vet. Considering the unusual blend of contents in the cat basket, the vet did not seem greatly surprised to see an active infant squirrel in the family. His attention quite properly was directed to the cat, and after injecting her and the kittens he gave a series of medicines and a special diet to try to restore the animals to health once more. He also examined Sammy but felt that he was in no danger providing that he had some alternative food supply now that Beauty's liquid resources had dried up. Having taken on one set of responsibilities, we now had another. There was no way of knowing whether Beauty would survive. Her coat became scraggy; she was limp and listless and she succeeded in ejecting all the fluid we tried to squirt down her throat. The two kittens also looked bad but they would at least take fluids. The next three days were crucial.

5 Over the Hump

Once more my home became a massive animal feeding station day and night. The cat could not be tempted with any food and the main problem, we were told, was the fear of dehydration. Somehow we had to get liquid into Beauty in order that her sense of taste and smell would recover, and only then would she get to the stage of even considering whether to eat. She was pitiful to look at and it seemed as if she would die anytime as she lay immobile, eyes closed, in her basket.

Although Beauty had no milk to offer, this did not stop the kittens and Sammy trying to force food from her nipples and so we took them away and let the mother have a rest from her maternal responsibilities. Sammy was kept with the kittens and they were housed in a separate box where the whole lot were fed on warmed cow's milk from a pipette just like our squirrel youngsters. The kittens took to the new diet without problems and by this time we had got pretty skilled at the art of hand feeding animals ourselves.

It was Philip Sharpe, a young technician at Oxford Scientific Films, who finally saw Beauty over the hump. With endless patience he sat by Beauty's basket (and the fleas) for the best part of two days, and encouraged her to take fluids. First only a few drops were forced down without her rejecting them and then later a little more. However, so weak had Beauty become that for another thirty-six hours she looked no better, even though more and more fluid was going into her system. Then suddenly some smelly fish was cautiously nibbled and over the next few days she gradually returned to her full strength.

During this time the kittens who had the 'flu became progressively worse, and so on 20 April a second visit to the vet was called for, once more taking Beauty with her family in their travelling basket. Again we took Sammy along for a check-up although his strength was evidenced by the fact that he would crawl up and look out of the viewing holes in the side and top of the cat basket while the one healthy kitten would claw around within. The vet looked concerned and gave all the cat family another 'flu injection, as well as some flea powder that he felt (but could not be sure) would remove the fleas from the cat but not harm the kittens or the squirrel. For a while we didn't try it. As it happens we were probably over-cautious but a few fleas seemed unimportant against the worry that we might lose our cat family or the squirrel.

Little by little, Beauty pulled through and after five days of illness the kittens and Sammy Squitten were feeding from her again. Once her coat had regained its gloss, she looked as well as we had ever seen her. Sadly that was not the case for all the kittens. One remained healthy throughout and was always the most lively of the bunch from then on. However the other two had the 'flu so badly that their eyes became blocked and, although they lived to become healthy cats, they each finished up with one slightly disfigured, cloudy eye. These were not so bad that it would be obvious but an experienced observer would have noticed the tell-tale 'squint'.

Now all of Beauty's family was back with her again, it was

possible to see how Sammy was making out with his step-kittens. All the youngsters were sufficiently small to be relatively helpless and the greater part of their time was still spent feeding and resting below Beauty's warm body.

It was always interesting when the mother cat left her family in order to go for food or to stretch her legs, because then we could see how the young animals were getting on. With increased strength they were beginning more and more to crawl around the nest, although it was amusing to see that they didn't lose touch with their nest mates for long before they would turn and try to bury themselves under the others. Sammy had two large teeth by now, and it seemed at first surprising that he could feed from the cat without causing her major injury. The two lower incisors at the front were massive and viciously sharp, but of course, in nature, those same teeth would have been present as the baby squirrel gripped the nipple of its own mother, and it presumably would cause no harm to her either. When he was distressed by, for example, a kitten competing for 'his' nipple or when being dried after a hand-feed, he would threaten by opening his mouth which revealed his lower teeth. Although none of his upper teeth had yet erupted, Sammy appeared at first sight to have both jaws armed with protective teeth. This effect was achieved by a simple patterning on the upper lip of a baby squirrel and I do not know if anyone has previously noticed it or speculated upon its function. There are two pale areas of skin below the nose which divide down to the upper jaw and closely resemble a pair of upper teeth. It may be significant that in adult squirrels this patterning disappears. It seems possible that baby squirrels have these mimic teeth to add to their threat potential when they are still suckling between the top of their tongues and the upper jaw without having teeth in the top jaw at that time. It is certainly true that some animals like weasels do attack young grey squirrel nestlings and this device of nature may help to deter such enemies.

Perhaps I should add that, at this time, Sammy always held out his tail like a rat's, that is hanging behind and showing no tendency to curl over in the typical adult squirrel manner. With his large claws and strong legs the squitten was in fact more exploratory initially than were the kittens. However, having dragged himself round to examine the edges of the cat basket he would still suddenly appear to feel vulnerable and would lose no time in turning back and burying deep into the darkness below all the other occupants. Were he to have been living in the wild, he would have similarly explored the confines of his drey but he certainly would not have ventured outside at this stage. As well as stoats and weasels, large birds of prey and other grey squirrels would possibly eat any youngster of Sammy's age if he were to leave the safety of the drey. However, in Britain the grey squirrel has few enemies other than man, unlike his native America where the species is eaten by various snakes, hawks and owls.

Beauty's response to Sammy remained the same. She would allow him to feed along with her own offspring; she would occasionally lick him but in general seemed only passively to accept the alien. To test this, I thought it would be interesting to see how she would respond if we removed Sammy and put him on the kitchen floor outside her basket. When we did this with any of the kittens, Beauty would watch intently and then move out and pick the wanderer up firmly but gently in her jaws and drop it back into the nest.

If the mother did 'recognise' Sammy as one of her brood, she would possibly react similarly when we took him out of the nest. However, we were a little concerned because, for the first time, it was likely that the cat would actually have the baby squirrel in her jaws. Would she, we wondered, suddenly react to it as a baby rodent and treat it as a desirable mouthful of food? There was the other possibility which was equally alarming. Could it be that the mother only considered Sammy to be a 'proper' part of her brood, while he was in her nest? Perhaps her instincts were to treat anything in her nest as her babies whereas once the youngsters were out of the nest they were viewed differently. This possibility was reinforced by our knowledge that mother birds treat any babies in their nests as their own, whereas once outside the nest, the parent bird will ignore its own young. This is what takes place when a young cuckoo hoists the rightful youngsters from a nest and the babies are then not recognised by the mother as her own chicks. If this happened with the squirrel and Beauty didn't view him as one of her rightful offspring, it seemed likely that she would simply see Sammy in a different light, would pounce and kill him.

Even if we did nothing, it was becoming clear that very soon our theories would be put to the test because Sammy was becoming more adventurous and was increasingly likely to drop out over the edge of the basket on his wanderings. So, one night after Beauty had had a good meal of her favourite cat food and was hopefully not interested in eating, we recovered Sammy from the warmth of the nest and placed him on the floor in front of the basket. Beauty immediately sat up on her haunches and stared intently at the pink squirrel. He started to crawl, following the curve of the basket, and Beauty moved her head from side to side and up and down as if uncertain what to do. Sammy squeaked his shrill alarm calls as he dragged himself over the kitchen floor and Beauty lifted her paw and made as if to step out after him. She licked her lips as she raised and lowered her head, obviously intensely aware of the struggling infant. It was difficult for us to infer what she intended to do, but we were close at hand ready to dash in if Beauty should fancy Sammy for her final course. However, after watching the ungainly pil-grimage of the plaintive animal, Beauty carefully stepped out of the basket, picked up Sammy gently in her mouth and returned to drop him next to his step-family. She licked him long and hard as Sammy tried to bury himself under the kittens and then she gave her attention to each of the kittens and licked them in turn. Finally, seemingly satisfied that all was well, she lay down over her family and we could hear the contented noise of suckling interspersed with her wheezy purring.

One more hurdle had been passed. We repeated this test twice on the next day prior to Beauty's feeding time and in each case the behaviour was identical. After a few minutes watching, the mother would reach out and retrieve the isolated squirrel from the floor. Within two more days, that became unnecessary for Sammy was developing so quickly that, using his already well-developed sense of smell, he was able to locate his family basket and using his claws and strong legs, he could readily climb back into the nest as Beauty watched. Whenever he returned from such a walkabout, she would treat him to a bout of licking.

Sammy was also increasingly active when he was not asleep or suckling on Beauty, and was always on the move. When still young, he would alter his position to find the warmth and contact of his family and when a little older, he would explore his environment in a series of minor journeys around the kitchen.

Everyone's life was made more pleasant by the application of our vet's flea powder. When all the animals were back to health following the 'flu scare, we cautiously tried small quantities of the powder in regions where the babies were not suckling. This made a big difference and, because there were no side effects on any of the youngsters, we gradually increased the dosage until the fleas had effectively disappeared.

Days passed and the family grew larger and stronger. It was about two weeks since Sammy had been introduced to the cats. Now when Beauty had left them for a time, the kittens started to stretch their claws and play with each other in mock fighting. As they began to co-ordinate paws and eyes, they would lie on their sides and indulge in mock boxing matches with each other or sit upright on their haunches and gingerly strike out at some part of

one of their neighbour's anatomy. Any kitten would respond in
a like manner, but Sammy's innate breeding or 'instincts' had
not prepared him for this sort of behaviour and he simply took
avoiding action by trying to bury himself out of the way. If he
was caught in the open, his movements of retreat would encourage several of the kittens to stumble after him and claw him
repeatedly as their hunting instincts began to assert themselves.

It was clear that the kittens' first impulse was to trap their
'prey' against the ground by placing a forepaw down somewhere on Sammy's body. Then they would lay on their sides
and 'hug' him around his chest with both forepaws while using
their hind feet to subdue all his other movements. In this position
they would keep practising their neck-biting skills, the one piece
of cat feeding behaviour that every kitten must learn for itself
by play fighting. It is in order to teach this lethal technique that
mother cats commonly bring a live mouse to their litter and
release it in front of their kittens while they 'play' with it
repeatedly – developing in the youngsters the essential knowledge of the proper place to bite.

At this stage Sammy didn't squeak or yell so it didn't seem to
hurt him. His only reaction was to take flight. He simply didn't
appear to want to play with the rough boys! Beauty never
moved to stop this treatment of Sammy – and neither did we for
it was evident that the kittens were still too small to do any harm
to our wiry squitten. What would happen later when the kittens
attacked in all seriousness? Only time would tell.

6 Growing Up

The biggest danger for Sammy came at a time when we least expected it. By 26 April Sammy had started to leave the basket completely and explore when Beauty herself left to stretch her legs. He still scuttled along with a somewhat rolling gait but at times he would begin to lift his tail up over his back. At this stage, his body was only just beginning to show a short covering of hair and the tail bore no resemblance to the characteristic fluffy banner of the adults. In fact, it was rather pathetic because, having hoisted his scrawny tail over his back, it would droop down obstinately as if the squirrel did not yet have the muscular strength to keep it there.

As they got older, the kittens became more and more intent on play-fighting and Sammy's tail became an object of fascination for them. He would often find himself unable to proceed because a playful paw was flattening his tail to the ground!

When all the family was out of the nest the kittens would begin to cuff and paw each other, each giving as good as they got. When they tried this on Sammy, he would tuck his head down and tolerate it for a while before suddenly skidding off on the smooth kitchen floor to hide under the sanctuary of the deep freeze.

As they became more and more mobile, the babies explored corners of the kitchen that the duster never reaches. One evening Sammy lodged himself inside the workings of the gas central heating boiler, only to emerge much later black with soot; it took about ninety minutes to bathe and dry him down again. The kittens too liked to play behind the oven or in the narrow corridors between the kitchen units and could only be coaxed out by one of us lying on our stomach and flipping a feather or a paint brush as an invitation to come out and play. Quite soon various parts of the kitchen developed barricades to keep the inquisitive youngsters out. Breadboards, cardboard boxes, trays and planks of wood were propped in the most unlikely situations to keep the family of filmstars out of mischief.

As their muscles developed the babies all became more active until on 29 April Sammy learnt to move more like an adult squirrel. The day was memorable because it was then for the first time that Beauty looked as if she might kill him.

From the moment we first saw Sammy he had been able to crawl along with his strong clawed feet although at first most of his body simply dragged along the ground. As he got older, he became stronger and walked along rather ponderously like most baby animals including the kittens. Then as he became more independent, he began to move in a manner more and more unlike the kittens. In particular Sammy started to run around in a rather erratic, random way, first running then quite suddenly stopping and then dashing off again. Mere words cannot convey this very typically squirrel-style method of progression but it was markedly different from the more regular, less jerky style of locomotion that the kittens adopted at this stage.

On that fateful evening, Beauty left her basket as I put down her food and as she did so, she pulled away from the members of her family who, until then, had been contentedly suckling beneath her. Finding themselves in the light and with no mother beside them, the group of youngsters broke up, climbed out of the basket and set out on their separate ways to explore. Suddenly Sammy realised what it was to be a squirrel and started to run around in his new squirrel style, quite differently from the three kittens. Beauty was distracted by Sammy's movements as she was eating and she turned to face him. Her eyes widened, her ears went back and her back stiffened and she was instantly in the posture of a cat alert to pounce. Sammy had paused and was having a good scratch before suddenly dashing off in a new direction. Beauty, her eyes flashing, tried to leap the yard or so to catch him but her feet slipped on the polished kitchen floor and she took several ineffectual skidding steps as she tried to reach him.

Although stunned, I was down on Beauty before she reached the young squirrel and, as I held her in my arms her attitude seemed to change to curiosity as she watched Sammy's new style of hopping. Her mood had passed as quickly as it had come and she simply looked on in a manner that, in a human, you would describe as being puzzled. Sammy was unaware that he had provoked Beauty to attack and he continued to proceed around the edge of the kitchen floor until he arrived immediately in front of Beauty. I loosened my grip and the cat gingerly pawed towards the squirrel as if unsure what to do. Then, lowering her muzzle, she sniffed at Sammy and then licked him.

Understandably we kept a very close eye on the family for the next few hours for we could see that Beauty kept an unusually alert interest in the squirrel's movements. However, in the event, it seemed that the incident was an isolated one, and that Beauty had learnt that the strange jerky mover was, in fact, one of her family. When all five animals returned to their basket, all appeared peaceful once again.

Two days later, Beauty was again momentarily provoked

into a hunting attitude by Sammy's antics but almost as soon as
she had bristled in anticipation she calmed down and studied her
strange orphan as he hopped on his way. From then on, Beauty
seemed to accept Sammy's essential 'squirreldom', without any
further adverse reaction.

As the young squirrel grew bigger and more adventurous, we
were entertained daily to new and amusing exploits. Once,
when the youngsters were left on their own in the basket, we
saw the growing kittens nipping and chasing Sammy as they lay
together on their blanket. Having tolerated days of having his
tail pulled and bitten, Sammy at last responded by turning his
head on one side and, hustling towards the attackers, started to
bite and playfully claw them in return. This retaliation was new
to the kittens and they lay back and pawed the air and bared their
teeth in gentle response. Soon energetic play fights were
common daily occurrences with Sammy giving as good as he
got. Invariably a kitten started it, but usually the encounter was
finished by Sammy using his front legs and mouth together to
suppress and repell the attacker. Often he would finish by
bounding off out of the way or climbing up on to a kitchen
chair, a skill which the kittens couldn't match. Watching the
youngsters at play, we felt that Sammy was indeed becoming a
squitten, having learnt to hunt and play in a similar fashion to his
step-brothers and sisters. I later showed our film to people who
had hand-reared baby squirrels and they agreed that, while
certainly playful, their youngsters never showed such cat-like
play hunting.

Some of the most delightful learning experiences of the
developing squirrel occurred quite incidentally with Sammy's
early discovery of Beauty's bowl of milk. Having crawled out in
an ungainly style from the basket, Sammy stumbled along the
kitchen floor until he hit the unyielding edge of the pottery bowl
holding his step-mother's drink. He lifted himself by putting his
front feet on the edge of the bowl and, opening his mouth, he

Above Sammy at a dinner party

Previous page Sammy learning to drink milk from the cat's bowl

Right Sammy burying a nut in the kittens' litter tray

Misbehaving at a dinner party

Right Fast asleep – John Paling and Sammy
(copyright: Tony Evans)

Sammy gives a demonstration of his nest-making skills, using an electric food-mixer bowl cushioned with tissues and an Income Tax envelope

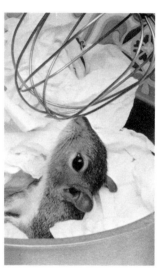

'The picture of total peace and self-righteousness . . .'

tried to suckle on the edge of the rim. His nose was under the milk and he snuffled and sneezed as he tried to master the art of drinking from a pool. His little tongue was licking at the outside of the vessel as he sucked hard and dunked his upper jaw into the milk. With a spluttering and shaking of wetted whiskers, Sammy was actually drinking very little milk at all. He raised himself on his haunches and succeeded only in submerging his nose all the more which caused him to shake himself so violently that his front feet slipped and he fell in the milk. Continuing to splash, choke and suck, he walked forward until his whole body was saturated in the drink. He was clearly out of his element and he finally crawled out bedraggled and located his basket, crawled up the wickerwork and on to the blanket. Beauty lost no time in licking him clean, no doubt getting a double satisfaction from her efforts.

It was not much longer before Sammy mastered the art of drinking from the milk bowl and although he continued to suckle on Beauty, he would nevertheless help himself to a drink of cow's milk whenever he stumbled across it. Later still, when he learnt to climb on tables he would always help himself to an unguarded cup of tea, and could usually be relied upon to climb into it and knock it over in the process!

When he was about three and a half weeks old, Sammy began to grow his upper teeth and we started to consider when to wean him on to solid foods. In nature, the young squirrel would begin to eat buds and leaves as he started to feed independently, and it was always our intention to release Sammy in due course, so we wanted him to be familiar with feeding on natural squirrel foods when the time came.

The signs that Sammy was beginning to feed independently came by chance as we observed that, in his increasing wanderings around the house, he began to pick things up and examine them in his front paws in a typical squirrel-like manner. An early find was a 'golden nugget' dropped from one of my boys' breakfast cereal bowl. Later the squirrel found one of the shelled peanuts that I had in my pocket which I kept for feeding to birds. He nibbled away at that until, after about a minute, only half of it was left.

Shortly after that Sammy was allowed to attend a dinner party we were giving. As this was to be a special occasion, he was allowed out separately from the rest of his family and he hopped around the table as we kept a cautious eye on him. He soon got into trouble and began to clatter over the spoons and to stick his nose into the wine glasses so we returned him to the floor. While we had a meal, he was given a few nuts in a bowl just to keep him occupied. It wasn't long before he had nibbled enough and he then picked up one of the remaining nuts in his mouth, went over to the leg of an armchair and scratched away at the carpet with his fore feet before pushing the nut on to the ground with his mouth. He then scuffled his front feet sideways towards the nut in a perfect attempt to bury it. Having completed this sequence of behaviour he returned to the pot and carried off another nut, this time to 'bury' it on the carpet by the edge of the fireplace.

It was most impressive as, in one moment, he had suddenly acted out the whole of the burying behaviour sequence that is so well marked and characteristic of adult squirrels. This was the very first time he had ever tried this and there was no possible way he could have been influenced by other squirrels (our own hand-fed squirrels were being looked after separately at Oxford Scientific Films by this time). In layman's language, Sammy had carried out a piece of totally unlearnt 'instinctive' behaviour which is deep in the breeding pattern of all grey squirrels. Observations and experiments on adult squirrels show that they all carry out this sequence of actions when burying their food. It is so inflexible that, even if the nut is removed half-way through the operation, the animal still carries on the whole cycle of actions even though there remains nothing there to bury!

Sammy's burying behaviour was obviously a strongly developed feature of all grey squirrels and our youngster did not need to perfect his technique. However, what was amiss was a sense of what were appropriate places to bury his excess nuts. It was amusing to witness Sammy carrying off food and going to great trouble to 'bury' it plainly in view in the corner of the room, in a crack in the kitchen tiles or by a foot. He would have to learn in time more 'sensible' places where food could be hidden. This skill did improve with time and we found later to our cost that he could show great determination in burying his food in places that were ideal for hiding things.

Such complicated behaviour sequences as food burying that are inborn and do not have to be learnt by individual animals, are usually essential to their survival. In the case of grey squirrels in the wild, the young animals have to face their first winter effectively alone and unless they put nuts aside in the autumn in advance of the times of hardship in the winter, they would certainly die. Thus it makes sense for nature to have developed in grey squirrels the 'instinct' to collect any food excessive to their immediate needs, to scoop a hole to drop it in, and then to cover it up by wiping the ground with sideways movements of the front feet. In nature, the time when this most commonly occurs of course is during the autumn when nuts drop from the trees in huge numbers. Nuts will keep fresh over the winter before they germinate in the spring and so squirrels have nutritious food available at a time when there is little else for them to eat.

The burying behaviour makes the nuts less available to the other competitors for the nut crop as they hunt mainly by sight. The wild squirrel locates his buried nuts by smell but he is thought to know which area to search in from memory. It seems that each squirrel will concentrate his burying in a particular area of his territory choosing places with slightly higher landmarks so he will still be able to recognise the general area after heavy falls of snow. Even so, many nuts still get left, and subsequently develop having been effectively planted by squirrels. But even if it does make good sense in theory for squirrels to have innate burying behaviour, it was still most impressive to see our little squirrel suddenly enact this particular sequence from out of the blue, or, more accurately, from the inherited repertoire of thousands of his ancestors.

Beauty continued to feed and groom her family and, as her kittens grew, she started to teach them how to use the litter tray for their toilet. The kittens would follow their mother into the plastic tray filled with proprietary cat litter and the youngsters seemed to watch and get the hang of how to scrape a hole, do what they have to do and then turn round and scratch more litter to cover their wastes. This too is possibly in part at least 'instinctive' behaviour but it did appear that the mother helped them dig and cover when the kittens were unfamiliar with the technique. However when Beauty tried to demonstrate her technique to Sammy, he was singularly unimpressed. When Sammy found his way into the litter tray, he was not one bit interested in matters of personal hygiene. Although Beauty would perform in his presence and look round subsequently, Sammy never tried to copy her toilet behaviour. Beauty would then sniff at the squitten as if to check if he'd done anything. But after a negative response, she would pause, look hard at Sammy and move off.

Many people ask how hygienic squirrels are to keep and whether they can be 'house trained'. In our experience, it is not possible to train them. Our animals all produced dry tubular droppings about a centimetre long. These were deposited anywhere the animal happened to be but they did have the virtue of not being messy and being easy to clear up!

So the litter tray was of no use to Sammy for his toilet needs but it was an ideal site for his developing burying behaviour. On finding an excess of food as he grew older, he would immediately run into the tray, dig with his paws, push the nut into the hole and hurriedly cover it up by sideways movements of his fore paws.

So great and urgent were Sammy's reactions that he was not considerate of whether his intentions conflicted with those of the kittens that might be using the tray. Whenever the drive came upon him, Sammy would seize a piece of food and barge into the tray, if needs be pushing aside any kitten that might be half-way through his private affairs. When this happened it was difficult not to interpret the kittens' expressions as being of pained irritation! Occasionally the multi-purpose facility of the litter tray caused unhygienic consequences as the kittens, probably unintentionally, got their own back.

This problem was overcome by not giving Sammy excesses of food and, later, by providing a straw-filled box where he could bury food to his heart's content.

There remains one memorial to Sammy's burying behaviour that only now can I look back on with a smile.

When he was about half-grown, on 15 June to be precise, I went out during the evening leaving Sammy free in the kitchen. He knew his way around the house by this time and was restrained from causing any trouble by an assortment of covers, basins, planks and trays that had been built up little by little to keep him out of mischief. He could easily climb up chair and table legs and gain access to all the work surfaces so the kitchen tended to have a permanent appearance of being under a minor siege.

On this particular evening I had planted some parsley seeds in an old pâté pot so that they might grow indoors in the winter and I had left them freshly watered on the window ledge. I returned late that night to find the whole place in a terrible mess. The wet soil had been dug out and there were piles of black compost and squirrel paw prints over the windows, along the work surfaces, over the oven and all over the floor. It was as if someone had been throwing mud pies everywhere and the culprit was not hard to identify as he came hopping out with filthy feet. It must have taken twenty minutes to clean the place up and to refill the pot with the aid of the kitchen spatula. The refilled bowl was then put out of reach on the top of the isolated deep freeze whose sides Sammy could definitely not climb.

Little more was thought of the incident at the time but later it became obvious that not one of the parsley seeds were growing. Instead, there emerged like a monster in a pool, a single broad sturdy stem with a pair of large leaves. It was a peanut plant! A little gentle excavation revealed that Sammy had planted a complete unshelled peanut at the very bottom of the bowl and this had now burst through the shell of the nut and was thriving in the pâté pot. I don't know why the parsley seeds all failed to grow but, no matter, the peanut plant grew large and strong as a tribute to Sammy's gardening ability.

This discovery was doubly amusing to us because one of my colleagues at Oxford Scientific Films, George Bernard, had been trying to grow peanuts for a long time for some book illustrations that he had been asked to do. He had planted about twenty, given them the best of attention and provided them with ideal conditions in our greenhouse – but he couldn't get a single peanut to grow. Among his other skills, therefore, Sammy could justifiably claim to have 'green paws'.

As Sammy's burying skills became better orientated, he would choose a dark crack in which to deposit his nut before burying it. This could lead to amusing consequences whenever we had guests. As ever, Sammy would steal all the attention and be the centre of attraction in the cat family. By now he was running around everywhere and readily jumped up visitors' legs. This could be a painful experience and was also costly on ladies' tights but Sammy was a seductive charmer and ladies particularly adored having him on their shoulders and feeding him. His rounded soft face and upright posture obviously brought out their maternal instincts. Sometimes at dinner parties, I would allow them the pleasure of having Sammy sit confidingly on their hand or shoulders while they cooed their admiration. Then, if he'd been fed, I would let them give Sammy a large unshelled peanut. As they watched, he could usually be relied upon to transfer it crosswise to his mouth, to trot along their bosom . . . and shove it down their cleavage!

7 Half-Way House

Just like a child, Sammy Squitten's development seemed to progress in fits and starts. The very first time he demonstrated his innate, instinctive behaviour of burying nuts (albeit on the carpet), he followed it on the same evening with his first attempt at collecting nest materials.

The dinner party we had given for Sammy seemed to bring out the best in him for, as if to impress all the other guests, he entertained us all at length with his nut burying tricks (now you see it . . . now you still see it; but I'm going to pretend it's gone). Then, seemingly possessed of an extra surge of energy, he hopped around the room alertly exploring anything he came across. His feet pattered over a copy of a newspaper on the floor and he paused at the edge sniffing into its open edges; then head down and squatting on his rear legs, he began to rummage backwards with his front paws, retreating as he did so. His sharp claws tore into the paper and produced something like a crumpled ball and this gave him more bulk of paper to work upon. This activity didn't last for long, and although only relatively few shreds of paper were finally pulled together, it was clear that he had constructed something which, in an adult, might become the basis of a nest. In those few actions, Sammy had demonstrated that this essential behaviour for collecting nest materials was something else that was inbred and could not possibly have developed from the teaching of Beauty and her kittens.

In the wild, all squirrels build dreys for themselves and this behaviour improves with experience as the year progresses. The typical domed nests of winter are basically made of leafy twigs and are lined with shredded leaves, bark and moss. Many of them are added to and repaired so that they are occupied for several years running. There is usually a single entrance hole to each one but this is often concealed on the side facing the trunk of the tree. This warm and waterproof house is so important for squirrel survival that once again it is not surprising that the basic skills of collecting nest material are born into every squirrel, including Sammy.

The strength and completeness of the nest-making skill was very clearly demonstrated one evening when Sammy was more independent yet still living with Beauty and her family. All the animals had been left on their own in the kitchen and the kittens were contentedly asleep in the basket but Sammy was nowhere to be seen. The door from the kitchen to the hall was not properly closed so our first task was to walk round the house hunting for possible places where Sammy had slept in the past. His favourite spot for a quiet snooze was a crevice between cushions on the sofa. On this occasion, he was not to be found there nor in other familiar places such as under the boys' beds in the end room, or in the dark under a chair. We then had to comb the house from end to end. He wasn't in the bedrooms, wasn't in the dining-room or hall but finally was located in a most unexpected place in the kitchen.

The clue to Sammy's whereabouts was an empty packet of paper tissues on one of the work surfaces. It had been half full when I'd left it but was now simply a shell of cardboard. Nearby was the culprit. Sammy was fast asleep in the bowl of the electric food mixer fully cushioned in the soft bedding made up of tens of sheets of white man-size tissues! To crown his bedroom décor, he had actually taken in my income tax form and its envelope and so was the picture of total peace and self-righteousness, his head resting on a chewed up legend, 'On Her Majesty's Service'!

So delightful was this sight that on another evening, we allowed him to repeat this nest building exploit but this time with the cameras on hand to document his actions. For most of that day, Sammy had rested with Beauty and the kittens and in the evening we watched as he had a good run round. Then, on the presumption that a full stomach would help turn Sammy's mind to thoughts of sleep, we fed him as many peanuts and acorns as he would eat. Soon he had lost interest in feeding and was running off with the nuts to 'bury' them in corners of the kitchen. Only then, did we put down an opened packet of paper tissues near the electric food mixing machine.

As soon as Sammy located the tissues, he scrabbled about with his front feet, his nose pressed into the tissues until he had scuffled two or three sheets into a concertina-like heap. Then, seizing the tissues with his teeth, he stretched his head back as he tried to pull them from the box. This was made the more difficult because he was still standing on them with his rear legs but with repeated upward jerks of his head, he freed a collection of sheets and ran over with them to the mixer bowl. He jumped on to the edge and pulled his trailing load inside. He released the white sheets and trampled them down before returning to collect more. As more sheets were removed, it became easier for him to pull out more of the tissues and, with head held high, he ran off with ever bigger mouthfuls. His burden made transport difficult for the tissues had to be trailed either between his legs or at one side of his body. When the paper got under his feet, he would stumble and his head would be pulled to the ground. If he was trying to jump up into the mixing bowl when this happened, he would be brought down short and would have to pick himself up and start again.

It took much more perseverance with the income tax form for the paper was stiffer and shiny. The squirrel tried several times but could not easily claw a crumpled patch into it so that he could grip it with his teeth. By chance he had better luck with the envelope for, having managed to grip it in his jaws, he dragged it laboriously to the bowl, the stiffness of the contents causing it to catch upon other obstacles on the kitchen work surface. Once it was in, however, he patted it into shape and it curved neatly around the inside of the nest.

Soon he had filled the bowl with tissues and had made a nest, relatively flattened at the bottom but with a loose covering on top, under which he settled down to sleep.

Now Sammy had shown that he was capable of making a nest on his own, we decided that the time had come to prepare him in earnest for a fully independent existence. After five weeks with us, we built him a separate home that was to be placed by the side of Beauty's basket so that he could begin to sleep apart from the family if he wished.

Scientists researching squirrels had already devised the most suitable size for their nest boxes, and so we built Sammy a wooden box exactly to those dimensions with an entrance hole two and a half inches in diameter. My plan was to let him get accustomed to this new home as a half-way stage. Later it would become his home in the wild.

We filled the bottom of the box with dry grass and intro-duced Sammy to our alternative accommodation to Beauty's basket. He didn't hesitate to enter and soon made himself at home going in and out, resting on the roof and then finally rustling down in the hay. When we lifted the observation lid to see how he was making out he leapt at us and snarled. Suddenly he had acquired a sense of unmistakable territoriality. He chattered his teeth loudly as a sign of anger and darted up at any hand or face that came towards him. So fierce was his response that we left him for a while to calm down before trying again.

Time wasn't any help, however. Sammy was just as violent an hour later and, as we needed to move him, we felt we had to oust him temporarily from the new home for which he had suddenly developed such a strong sense of protection. By the simple device of lifting off the lid and tipping the box upside down, the complaining squirrel was deposited unceremoniously on to the kitchen table.

Once away from the box, his attitude calmed again and we could handle him without problems. However, it struck us that it was no bad thing for our young squirrel to show a strong defensive streak. He was going to have to be tough and assertive if he was going to survive in the wild in a few weeks' time.

So we were in no way daunted and made Sammy's hay bed before placing the nest box down by Beauty's basket for the night. The family sniffed around the new furniture and Sammy popped in and out of the nest hole as if to reclaim his property.

Since we were now moving towards setting Sammy on the road to freedom, we decided at the same time to start feeding him leaves and buds that young squirrels in the wild would now be eating. So for that evening meal, two dishes were put down side by side. In front of Beauty's basket there was the usual cat food (which the kittens were also starting to eat now) and in front of Sammy's box was presented a vegetarian's special of oak, sycamore and beech buds. As the dishes approached, all the animals left their different homes. Each explored the other's menu and soon they settled down to feed as nature had intended, the squirrel sitting back on his haunches eating leaves and the cats eating their tinned meat.

That night we allowed the animals to sleep where they chose and we were pleased to see that Sammy settled himself down in his nest box, while Beauty's kittens were still faithful to her and nestled down to suckle after their evening romp.

Next morning I was up earlier than the animals and I went straight into the kitchen to see how they had made out. Beauty was curled up in her basket and looked up with half an eye open while still resting her head on her paws. I tapped the squirrel box gently and heard a rustling within. A scratching on the wood was followed by a head being poked from the hole. It was Charlie, one of the kittens! He heaved himself out from the box and was followed by Pickles and only then by Sammy who seemed in a good mood for he showed no sign of aggression once he'd left the box. The remaining kitten, Scruf, was still sound asleep under Beauty. Evidently during the night Sammy had allowed his family to share his much-guarded territory without any sign of there having been a struggle. From then on, Sammy spent most of his nights in his box in the company of one or other of his step-kittens. During the day he would spend time still suckling with Beauty but already all the youngsters were showing more independence. The mother too was spending more and more time away from her family until some days she would appear to deliberately get out of their way by walking off and hiding under a chair or bed. The time was approaching when the members of the family would go their separate ways.

Sammy's new diet came to make up a bigger and bigger proportion of his daily intake and, like similarly aged squirrels in the wild, he sampled many new types of potential food. This was demonstrated to us by one more night of chaos in the home caused by Sammy.

By now, half the house was barricaded off to limit Sammy's access to potentially troublesome situations. But some parts had to stay untouched to maintain the basic civilities of living. We didn't take the curtains down for example, although he would still run up and behind those; we didn't remove the pictures although he occasionally played see-saw along the tops of their frames. And we didn't remove the flowers although he finally discovered a taste for any vegetation in the house.

Few things are more beautiful than an arrangement of roses and to our astonishment, Sammy found them very appealing too; only his interest was to eat them. The first we knew of this aberration was to find a bowl overturned on the coffee table and the chewed up contents scattered far and wide. As usual, the squirrel was nowhere to be seen when the chaos was discovered but was located sleeping soundly alongside the kittens and Beauty. He hadn't eaten the hard stems, we found, but the petals and leaves.

Once again, we felt that this episode was something too good to miss for the film so we arranged to be on hand when next Sammy was let loose on a bowl of flowers. We obviously had to decide what flowers to use for the filming session. Somehow roses didn't seem the most appropriate diet for a squirrel so we decided to let Sammy make the choice for himself by taking him to the local florist for a sampling session!

The lady in charge of the flower shop in Woodstock town is a kind and tolerant soul who received us with a dry smile when I explained our request. To the delight of the staff and the incredulous customers, Sammy was let loose to take his pick. Asparagus fern was popular; so were chrysanthemums, corn-flowers, asters, daisies, roses – in fact virtually everything he sampled was chewed up with relish. It was obvious that he would eat the petals and leaves of any arrangement we put together. Naturally we didn't wish to hazard his health so I tried chewing a selection of the flowers too, in case any seemed too strong or noxious to risk on Sammy. Of his choice I found chrysanthemums the strongest so we planned to stop him eating those even though we used them for the bowl. (None of the flowers tasted as bad to me as horse chestnuts which wild squirrels will eat without problems.)

The scene was set. The flowers looked at their best and Sammy was set down to do his worst – and he did! He immediately ran over to the arrangement and sniffed the flowers. A rose happened to be the first to go followed by some ferns, a taste of cornflower and, then, with a jerk, the whole lot was knocked over. Before he finished, he had chewed at most of the vegetation and, amidst the debris, 'for afters' Sammy chewed into the green foam that was used to hold them all in place.

Our squirrel had reached the stage where Beauty's milk was hardly necessary for him and, on the advice of the cat's home, we finally settled that the kittens could now also look after themselves. Although we wanted to hang on to all the youngsters for another few weeks, we felt that the time had now come for Beauty to leave us and be returned into the tender care of Mrs Gray. So on 28 May, we put Beauty all by herself into the travelling basket and drove her back to the sanctuary, where she was immediately welcomed once again into the company of the other animals.

Beauty had served us and her strange family extremely well. She was a devoted and patient mother who looked after not only her three kittens but also the total alien that we had introduced to her. It is likely that Sammy quite literally owed his life to her, for about half of the original cluster of orphaned squirrels which we had adopted died, despite our best efforts to keep them going.

Of the six animals (excluding Sammy) that we hand-fed throughout, two of them survived to adulthood. Philip Sharpe later took on the burden of maintaining the bottle-fed brood and weaned them on to a diet of nuts and leaves. In the final stages they were given a squirrel box of their own and this was finally put up into a tree in the small wood in my garden with the animals inside. The opening of the nest hole was unblocked and the animals were free to take their chance in the wild after fifty-four days of being brought up by humans. The next animal to be released would be Sammy Squirrel.

8 Havoc

Early days with Sammy were pure bliss compared with the un-imaginable chaos that often surrounded him as he grew older.

It started in little ways that could be almost amusing were it not for the fact that more and more damage was being caused. A favourite squitten game was hide and seek under and over the armchairs and sofa in the sitting-room. It was usually started by the kittens being fascinated by Sammy's fluffy tail and their attempts to pounce on it. This was a signal for Sammy to scuttle away up the upholstered furniture keeping his body flat, close against the surface. The kittens would bound up after him and the squirrel would keep in hiding over the brow of some curve of the furniture. (Wild squirrels do this around a tree trunk to keep out of sight from an approaching human.) The kittens would follow on, but were far less agile and were not the equal of Sammy's versatile limbs and claws. Because squirrels can rotate their rear ankle joints through 180°, they can easily walk down surfaces head first. Sammy would not only run down the back of the chairs but he would hang on and go all the way underneath upside down to emerge in triumph at the other side to the total bewilderment of the kittens. But very soon the claw marks and the snags began to show on the material until at the end of our association with Sammy, the whole lounge suite needed re-covering.

He could also cling on to jeans easily and he soon developed a skill for jumping up from the ground and climbing rapidly up one's legs on to the back or shoulders. On the back, he was clever enough to position himself at the very point where one simply could not reach with either hand from above or below despite all manner of contortions and gyrations. A variation of this leg-climbing behaviour was to take the less obvious route and to shin up the inside of the trousers. As he got higher up the garment, he could presumably feel the comfortable security of contact with leg and fabric on both sides of his body and he would force his way up as high as he could go. At this point, the only way he could be extracted was for the victim to retire and to take down his or her trousers and to recover Sammy from above!

Once Sammy realised the use of human legs as a convenient route to a comfortable perch on a shoulder, he would leap up on the calves even if the victim happened to be a lady not wearing trousers but nylon tights instead. This invariably resulted in snagged nylon and intolerably sharp claws scratching deep into sensitive human flesh. Soon all visitors learnt to arrive clad in thick jeans. Any delicate garments would be snagged by Sammy's powerful feet as he clambered over all the visitors.

The same was true for my velvet curtains which proved to be ideal for baby squirrel feet to grip on to. Net curtains in the hall were even better and left a pretty pattern of distortion effects where the claws had snagged the material. The little bit of gnawing he did at the chair legs was not really noticeable but when he chewed up the putty and part of a wooden window frame, the bills began to trickle in.

The teeth of a grey squirrel are used for many more purposes than to chew food and threaten. Very commonly a squirrel will pick something up and bite it as a way of investigating what it is. This, I am sure, was the simple intention of two semi-wild adult squirrels that have sat on my shoulder and gently pressed their incisors through a finger and an ear. Their teeth are razor sharp and go through human flesh very easily so it was important that Sammy learnt not to bite the humans he came into contact with.

Naturally as our young squirrel grew more versatile, he began to explore his surroundings and to use his teeth more and more in different ways. Whenever he bit one of us, we tapped him gently by way of reprimand, and although this would happen one or two times a week, Sammy did seem to get the message and never caused more than a few drops of our blood to be shed.

The most dramatic of Sammy's exploits could well have killed him and at the same time set fire to our building. One evening or early morning while Sammy was free in the house on his own, he decided to explore the electricity cables in the room. He chewed down to the base wires the two-core, thin white cable of a table lamp for about two inches of its length and, even more impressively, munched through a thick three-core flex that served the electric fire. How he didn't arc-weld his teeth together, is still a miracle. We were horrified at his potential for causing a major disaster and we realised we were all very lucky that nothing more serious had happened from his wire chewing. You can see why people in America fear that someday a squirrel may launch a rocket by nibbling at a cable. We knew already their gnawing has cut off the power to forty thousand people in St Louis so it was clear that we now needed to be doubly careful for Sammy could so easily have exposed two wires that would have sparked together and lead to the house catching fire and Sammy being transformed into 'squirrel oxide'!

Alarmed at the prospects, we transferred Sammy, and the kittens, to a store room at our studios at Oxford Scientific Films. All cables were removed, and the family home, bedding, food

Exploring the nest-box with the help of the kittens

Previous page Introducing Sammy to his nest box when he was 5 weeks old

Sammy 'appreciating'
a flower arrangement

Sammy causing chaos

Left Chewing the electric flex from a table lamp *Below* A close-up on squirrel damage

Sammy in his 'room at the top' preparing for his freedom

Sammy and Ivan fighting

and drink were re-established. For three days Sammy was allowed to stay there until he was found to be the villain of another drama.

Like most companies these days, Oxford Scientific Films has a comprehensive system of magic beams, alarm bells and security circuits to ensure that the place is not burgled. What's more, our system incorporated the added sophistication of a device which telephones an alarm to the nearby police station when any of the devices are set off or if any of the telephone wires are tampered with. Every evening, before the place is locked up, the circuits are all checked and a green light confirms all the safety devices are working before the final switch is thrown to put the emergency call system through to the police.

One evening we couldn't make the green light work and that usually indicated that either a door or window was not closed, or something had gone wrong with the electronics. There are so many things to check that the last person out usually has to stay on an extra half-hour or so trying to locate the fault before he finally resorts to locking the studios without the security of the electronic surveillance system.

Next morning the service engineer arrived in his white coat and moved from room to room checking that all the windows were shut and that electrical contacts on all the doors and locks were sound. When all these proved to be working properly, he began to wonder if something was wrong with the control boxes. After a whole day of tedious testing the system unit by unit, he still couldn't locate the trouble and for a second night the building was left unguarded. The next morning he returned and finally sorted out what had been the cause of the system breaking down. Sammy had eaten through the electrics again!

Each of those windows that do not open is circled with a band of metal stuck flat on to the glass in case someone tries to break in by cutting a hole in a pane of glass. This would disturb the band of metal and its circuit and set off the whole security system.

Sammy and the kittens were asleep at floor level when this discovery was made and, when we looked down at the culprits, they all looked the picture of innocence as they twitched and sniffed in their dreams. The service engineer seemed to find the whole thing very amusing which was more than my colleagues did when we got the bill to pay for his visit!

As it was only at the bottom of the glass near the window ledge that Sammy had reached, we covered the lower part of the metal band with broad, strong tape. With the episode behind us the building was once more secure at night. That evening for a change the green 'all checked' light functioned normally and the whole of our property again had an operational security system.

As it happened, we were incredibly lucky that the system was mended when it was for, by an amazing coincidence, that very night someone tried to break into the company's studios. The alarm system mercifully worked perfectly this time and the first I knew about it was by a 'phone message from the police station. They had been called by the automatic alarm system and a police car was on the way. Would I go to unlock the building while they surrounded the outside?

Dressed in an ill-assorted collection of clothes, I arrived in the car park to find the police car already inside the drive. From out of the gloom emerged two tall constables who had already made a discreet check all round the outside and even climbed the nearby bank to see if there was anyone on the roof. There was no trace of how the intruders had got in so we quietly unlocked the outside door and began to explore. Nothing seemed to be amiss. We switched off the alarm system and checked room by room. It began to seem as if it was a false alarm. Then, next door to the library, we surprised the culprit – Sammy.

He was actually hopping around on a table but I could see that he had again chewed at the band of metal on the window but this time had lifted only part of the tape. Although the law would never have known, I could see at a glance that this nibbling was enough to have disturbed the metal below and to trigger off the electrical warning system.

The policemen stopped and admired the cute squirrel. I explained that he lived with the cat and kittens and was being featured in a film . . . but somehow I omitted to mention that he eats security systems. The result of Sammy's gnawing was not obvious to a newcomer admidst the general clutter of the storeroom and before we left, we checked carefully and confirmed that the other openable window had been properly secured and so was not the cause of the security system going off.

Surprisingly we completed our circuit of the building and found that no one had in fact broken in. 'The security system must need mending,' I rightly concluded, 'it does occasionally go on the blink. I'll get the fellow to fix it tomorrow.' Which of course I did. By the time he arrived, a special big cage was being prepared out on the roof for Sammy!

9 Room at the Top

There was not much damage that Sammy could do inside a 15′ × 10′ × 10′ wire cage. Within this enclosure he had his own special sleeping box as well as access to a small wooden shed for his added comfort and protection. One side of the cage shared a common wire wall with the top of the big squirrel enclosure and so he soon got used to the sight and smell of adult squirrels next door. The kittens too were put upon the roof with him, having a choice of sleeping quarters either inside the shed or sharing Sammy's box.

In a way the 'room at the top' was a useful half-way stage prior to setting Sammy free. He was now exposed to fresh air every moment of the day and so could acclimatise himself to a life style away from human habitation and without the protection afforded by being housed indoors. He took to the change of environment without any signs of discomfiture. In fact, because we filled the enclosure with fresh branches and covered the roof with soil and planted grass and hedge bank vegetation all over the floor, he was suddenly in his element.

We made sure that he had fresh water and fresh oak, sycamore

and grasses and stems and at the same time we stopped anyone
handling him or feeding him directly to try to eradicate any
tendency for Sammy to associate humans with food. Obviously
if he was to be successfully returned to the wild, he must not go
seeking human company for his meals. So totally did Sammy
take to the life in the 'semi-wild' environment that he seemed to
us to be adapting very well and becoming a free roaming
squirrel. He hunted, hid and fed amongst the vegetation and
virtually ignored the kittens in his enclosure, living as he did
mainly high up along the branches and the upper reaches of the
wire netting. Within a week of transferring him to the 'room at
the top' Sammy was effectively avoiding the kittens and leaving
them behind him. He now did not need their warmth to see him
through nights in his box under the stars.

Like Beauty before them, the kittens were taken away from
their unique kittenhood companion and we found homes for
them with human foster parents. Pickles, who to me was always
the fittest and prettiest kitten and was something of an aristocrat
by temperament, was claimed by Mary, our secretary at Oxford
Scientific Films. Scruf, who was always getting into mischief
and was more rumbustious and friendly than either of the
others, was willingly mothered by Maureen, one of the young
assistants with the company. Both animals are now adult cats
living happily with their owners on a farm in the Oxfordshire
countryside. The third kitten, Charlie, was returned to Mrs
Gray at the cat's home. She was there for a short while before
being found an excellent home. Mrs Gray wisely did not use the
'as seen on TV' sales tag for that could possibly attract the wrong
sort of owner. Like all ladies too, Charlie would surely have
preferred to be wanted for her own sake – not as an appendage to
some man or his unusual project!

So Sammy was now all alone in the world. His coat was
beginning to change colour from a brown-grey to a light grey
shade. This was particularly evident on his tail and flanks where

there were clear tones of the two distinct colours. He fed and grew and on several occasions was seen taking mouthfuls of chewed up grass stems into his nest box to add to the insulation within. Clearly the behaviour pattern he had practised with paper tissues was now being put to proper use using the same techniques as any normal squirrel.

He would often not bother to come over to the door of the cage when I climbed up the step ladder and paid him a visit. He was also developing a reluctance to be caught and when situations did arise when we wished to capture him, he would typically scurry off and try to avoid us. All this was just what we wished to see.

As the weeks passed we began to prepare more and more for the time when Sammy would be set free. We wondered whether to let him go right out in the wild in the depths of the Wychwood Forest or whether to release him close at hand where we could keep an eye on him and ensure that there would be special supplies of nuts put out for him in the winter if the need arose. (I had developed a special squirrel feeder the previous year which when hoisted high up a tree, enables squirrels to get at the nuts and yet birds do not enter.)

Naturally we did want to follow his progress after release if at all possible and so I had to decide whether the woodland of my garden bordering the 1,200 acres of Blenheim parkland (including part of the old Wychwood Forest) was a suitable site for Sammy's new home base.

I only had to look outside my window and the reassurance I needed for that decision was hopping around almost every day. Those baby squirrels that had been hand-fed had been released previously into the trees of my garden and these I saw several times a week. They were noticeably tamer than wild squirrels but they wouldn't let me approach nearer than ten or fifteen feet before running away into hiding. They had no problem in keeping alive and healthy for they seemed to be in the peak of condition and obviously had not been forced to leave the area to find sufficient food.

But Sammy might be different, I pondered. His upbringing had been even more curious and might have made him less able to cope in the wild. For example, how would he respond to human pets if he encountered them? That question was answered for me very forcefully one evening.

As an exception to my rule, I had arranged to take Sammy to a friend's house so that he could take some photographs of our celebrity before he was released into the wild. My friend had had a serious illness and I felt totally justified in sharing my pleasure in Sammy's success story with him in the circumstances. I caught Sammy and held him in my hand as I climbed down the enclosure ladder and then walked through OSF's lobby towards my car. There I met my colleague and fellow director, David Thompson, who was just returning from walking his beautiful black labrador, Ben. The dog has a wonderful temperament and is admirably trained so he immediately sat on David's command. We spoke for a few seconds and then suddenly Sammy got the smell of Ben and went berserk. He struggled in my hand, his sharp claws ripping my fingers apart. He bit into the base of my thumb and I simply couldn't hold him! While Ben just cocked his ears and lolled his tongue in amazement, the squitten leapt off and climbed the window frame in the far corner of the lobby. The dog had shown no attempt to attack or threaten the squirrel but clearly Sammy's instincts were well attuned to possible danger from this unknown beast. Bleeding slightly I retrieved Sammy while David took Ben elsewhere and then I went on to visit my friend's home. There, the same problem occurred. Although the resident cat had been banished for the evening, Sammy smelt its scent and tried to get away from the place.

This all seemed to further our opinion that Sammy was rapidly taking up his instincts for the wild. When we thought of it, it was not too surprising for many other people over the years had brought up squirrels by hand and, despite daily contact and their owner's best endeavours, virtually all their squirrels turned wild as adults, and finally had to be caged separately, given to zoos or released. The notes from innumerable would-be squirrel keepers are festooned with telling observations of such incidents, 'bit my mother-in-law on the ear and then attacked the other house guests'; 'insisted on leaping on visitors' heads and chewing the curtains – we had to cage it', etc. It must be agreed that squirrels don't make good pets as adults. They all seem to have a persistent streak that defies domestication even for people who have brought their squirrels up by bottle-feeding and have had daily contact since they were helpless babies.

The final test we wanted to try was to see how Sammy responded to other grey squirrels. Scientists have long known that ordinary young squirrels have great difficulty finding a territory in the wild, for the older, more dominant, animals chase them away. The young males, particularly, move con-siderable distances to new areas which often seem less suitable for providing an adequate food supply.

As the dominant wild males will fight savagely to ensure a newcomer stays well down the 'pecking order', the fear was that even if Sammy was released in my garden he might get chased off immediately by one of the local 'old-timers'. He might then get pushed out to some less suitable area, possibly into other gardens with no suitable woodland cover and insufficient food or, even worse, on to the roads where so many are killed each spring and summer by cars.

As we had our vast enclosure available from our unsuccessful squirrel breeding programme, we didn't have far to go to test how Sammy would fare when introduced for the very first time to adult wild squirrels. At this time there were still seven animals living together in the hollow oaks. They all knew their place and the less dominant ones always gave way to those which were higher in rank to them. At the top of these squirrels' social pinnacle was a huge male, Ivan, who stood no nonsense from any other animal in the cage. He always had an immaculate fluffy coat, was fat and strong and bore sizeable evidence of his masculinity. So fierce was this creature that we were all terrified of it and on occasions had to enter the enclosure armed with an old badminton racket to protect ourselves from his attacks. He would approach fearlessly with tail down flat across his back, flicking the tip towards any intruder and chattering his teeth audibly in threat. The other squirrels knew him from past experience so now all he had to do was to advance and show himself and every other creature – including us – would be put to flight. (It is interesting to note that this male had been found as a tiny baby when its mother had been squashed by a car. It had been hand-fed by a young lady in Oxford and lived as part of her household for several months until it turned wild and began to attack people. When we came across it, it was being maintained in solitary confinement in a large cage and the animal could no longer be trusted even by his owner.)

Clearly with such a brutal and self-assured animal in the cage, we had to avoid Sammy being savaged and killed by this in-credible hulk. We had nicknamed him 'Ivan the Terrible'. We planned to introduce Sammy to his true kith and kin at a time when the big male was out of the way, having had a good feed and disappeared for his afternoon nap. Sammy had been in smell contact with all the other animals already and he was now brought down from his room at the top and held in a side enclosure while we fed the adults until they had had their fill. Naturally the boss took most of the nuts and, having filled his stomach, he buried a few of the remainder before disappearing into his hole in the trunk of our giant oak.

While two of the smaller females were still hunting for any remaining food in the long grass, we quietly opened the door and took Sammy in. He didn't appear at all concerned to be in a new environment and boldly started to sniff around the ground for food or for scent messages left by the other occupants. The two adults kept an eye on Sammy but did not approach him – possibly because I was near him in the cage with a racket to protect us in case Ivan should reappear! Sammy's nose located some of the nuts that had been buried and he sat on his haunches munching away as if he was perfectly at home there. It seemed as if we were in for a long wait before either of the females was going to come over and check out Sammy.

But our attention was suddenly diverted by the scratching sound of feet rapidly descending over oak bark as Ivan appeared on the scene bristling his greeting to the newcomer. Naturally I rushed up to separate the two but my movements sent Sammy running away from me, followed determinedly by a high-stepping Ivan. There was nothing I could do. Sammy was seemingly enjoying his freedom and, having no idea what the dominant male squirrel was capable of doing to him, he was more concerned to keep out of my way than to avoid Ivan. To chase him further could easily have resulted in Sammy running up the trees and inside one of the holes and anything could happen in there. It seemed better to leave Ivan to sort him out in a place where Sammy could at least demonstrate his submission by running away.

I looked on horrified as Sammy stopped to feed, sitting pertly on his rear legs and holding his food in his hands while Ivan moved mercilessly into battle. His fur was extended magnifi-cently, his tail rigid and flat along his back, his head was held low and his teeth chattered ferociously. He paused a foot away from Sammy and shook the tip of his tail prior to leaping in for his first bite. The intensity of his threat was totally unmistakable.

Except, of course, to Sammy Squitten who had not had the benefit of a normal squirrel education, where the language of the species would have been taught to him by his parents and by encounters with his brothers and sisters. All Ivan's posturings were completely meaningless and simply ignored by Sammy who had now finished his nut and set out to seek another. It was then that Ivan pounced. He grabbed at Sammy's back and his jump knocked Sammy off his feet.

What happened next is indelibly fixed in my mind. For although Sammy knew nothing of normal squirrel etiquette when in the company of dominant males, what he did know a lot about was fighting his own battles with three strong and energetic kittens!

Ivan the Terrible could not have known what had hit him. In no time at all, Sammy had him flipped over on his side and gripped between his forepaws, his teeth bared. Considering it was so long since Ivan had been even challenged, he remembered very quickly how to run away. With Sammy hot in pursuit, the much larger male streaked away jumping from stump to stump and through the long grasses in an attempt to shake off the nimble junior. Ivan's neat coat was now dishevelled and he had lost all trace of dignity as he raced off with his tail flat and sticking out like exhaust smoke behind him.

After less than a minute, Sammy was back searching for another nut while Ivan watched him with respect from high up a tree. In his naïvety Sammy had done something that we had all totally failed in. What is more he had settled a personal score for my young assistant, Philip, who, several months previously, had had Ivan bite through his finger to the bone and then hang on like a Christmas tree decoration on a branch.

Sammy was a hero and was returned to his own cage and nest box with great rejoicing. Clearly we had no need to worry further about releasing him. Sammy would not easily be beaten by a mere squirrel!

Part Two

10 The Release of Sammy Squirrel

We now planned to release Sammy into the wild on Thursday, 13 July. By this time he had been left predominantly on his own in a big cage and fed only with buds and shoots, particularly sycamore and oak trees, so hopefully he was used to the idea of feeding himself.

When the time came, we planned to take Sammy's wooden nest box outside and fasten it high up a tree in my wood so that at least out in the wild there would be a base he could return to and smell as being his own territory. What's more, I stocked some unshelled peanuts in the box so that if Sammy was initially unsuccessful in finding his own food, at least there was a supper left for him at home. Naturally we hoped that he would return to the box and continue to use it as his nest and sanctuary.

The thirteenth was a warm, mildly sunny day with hardly any wind. We decided to release Sammy in the late afternoon so that he would have plenty of time to explore his immediate surroundings but not be away too long before darkness descended when he would have to find shelter for the night.

Among my fears was the possibility that Sammy would move far away, excited by a sudden sense of freedom.

The two-sectioned aluminium ladder was extended full-stretch high up a tall beech tree in my garden. Sammy's box was lifted carefully into place. Inside Sammy had been somewhat unceremoniously locked in by the simple expedient of pushing an old tea towel into the entrance as a temporary restraint. With a few bangs the box was secured to the tree and with hardly a moment's pause the cloth was pulled away and I climbed down the tree. It didn't take long for Sammy to shoot out into the light to discover a new world. In fact he emerged with a peanut held in his mouth, which he leisurely proceeded to eat after climbing on to the lid of the squirrel box; having finished it, he seemed to smell the fresh open air around him and began to explore the immediate vicinity. He scampered eagerly and excitedly along the branches, but then ran back again and returned to the box reappearing almost as quickly with another peanut, which he consumed on the lid as before.

He returned probably five or six times in rapid succession, and then set off up to the very top of this particular tree which must have been fifty or sixty feet high. We could see him silhouetted against the blue sky until he was at the very topmost branch of what was, by any standards, a very tall tree. He seemed to survey the endless extremities of his new horizons, and then having satisfied himself perhaps that there was no longer any wire around him, descended into the thick of the tree to make a meal of some of the beech leaves.

Slowly but surely he moved on to one branch and then on to the others, occasionally retracing his steps, clearly sniffing the air all the while, to pick up the scent of whatever other animals had been in the vicinity. He moved from beech to sycamores and on round the garden until he must have covered fifteen different trees over no more than thirty or forty feet. The particular garden I occupy is ideal in many ways for all types of wildlife. It is an old quarry – the old walls of which surround the house and beyond them lie the open fields and parklands of Blenheim estate.

Because of the liberal supply of food I had put out over many years, there were at least the two squirrels in my garden – about the size of Sammy – which we had released previously and they seemed to be thriving well. In addition at least one adult regularly used my garden as part of its territory.

Sammy showed no inclination to come down to us. Clearly he relished his freedom and had no wish to return to human hands. Just to test this, at one stage I went under his tree and called him for a long time, holding nothing in my fingers but clicking them as if I was about to give him a peanut. If our training had been successful he would not return to this lure, because the one thing we wanted to avoid was that he should associate people with food. If he were to do so he would certainly become too trusting and would start visiting the neighbours, and possibly even bite them in frustration if he wasn't given the food he was seeking.

Finally, as dusk approached, Sammy's slow progress around the garden seemed to come to an end. High in a sycamore tree he built a thicker mass of leaves. To call it a drey would be a presumption, because it was little more than three or four twigs seemingly bent together to make a thickening on which he could sit. As dusk turned to darkness, there was no sign of further movement. I felt quite hopeful that he would in fact survive his first night in total freedom. I could do no more than leave him under the watchful eye of his creator and trust that no harm would befall him during the night.

The night was fine and dry, and next morning it did not take long to spot Sammy clambering among the sycamore trees. He showed no interest in approaching me, but went higher up into the tree when I approached. This was a very good omen. I watched him as he climbed from one tree to another, nibbling

occasionally, sometimes running up and down almost in play
and then finally reaching the top of the quarry wall, for a time he
disappeared over it into the parklands of Blenheim. Half an hour
later he returned and this time he was on a different tree in a
different part of the garden, quite low down. As I approached
him he stopped and watched me. He was about four feet above
the ground and in some strange way for the first time since he
had been released I felt that he did not any longer consider me as
something to be avoided. Somehow being so near to the ground
seemed to put him in a familiar relationship to me, and, as I stood
still, to my mixed feelings of delight and concern, Sammy
hopped down from the tree into the ivy and voluntarily leapt on
to my jeans, on to my back and so on to my shoulder. He didn't
get any food and I don't think he expected any. I had no
intention of encouraging him to return to me.

I walked with him on my shoulder twenty or thirty feet
towards the big beech tree where his box was so he might run up
that and re-establish himself there. He jumped off on the way
round; I didn't do anything to restrain him and quite soon he
was once more on the base of a different tree. I watched for a
while as he observed me – neither running away nor coming
closer – and then I approached him to within three or four feet,
and once again he hopped off the tree on to the ground, up my
leg and shinned up until he sat on my shoulder. This time he let
me walk with him to the big beech and as I brushed my shoulder
against the bark he simply jumped on to the tree. Within a few
minutes, he had popped inside his nest box and reappeared at the
hole to eat one of the peanuts from his reserves before climbing
high into the branches.

As the day wore on he moved once again right the way round
the edge of the garden until he reached one of the old willow
trees and then he finally came down to the ground in the dark
shadow on the lawn. For the first time I saw a second squirrel
there which must have been one of the other babies and was

about Sammy's size. Then one of them began a minor skirmish –
it was impossible to see which – running off at a great rate of
knots round the lawn, up the trees, and finally once again high
into the beech. For the next ten minutes there was a wild chase. I
was not able to tell from their size in the depth of the foliage to
see who was chasing whom but I think it was Sammy who was
being chased off by the local youngster from the community.
For a time, they both disappeared but then Sammy once more
turned up and carried on his lone track around all the trees until
he was again in the willow tree in the corner.

Time and time again he shinned up the high branches, chewing an odd leaf here and there, until he seemed to have explored
the whole area very thoroughly, particularly an old starling's
box, now empty, the remains of the nest presumably still within.
It crossed my mind, in fact, that the box might well have been
the site of one of the resident baby squirrels, because Sammy
made no attempt to stay there.

He finally made his way along to the bank at the top of the
quarry and disappeared for some hours. Although we searched
the nearby area, he was nowhere to be found. I was not greatly
worried as I guessed that Sammy had simply settled down for a
rest period. When he'd been in captivity his pattern of behaviour
was such that by midday, having been on the go since the start of
the day, he would certainly have been ready for at least a four-
hour snooze.

During the following day, I saw Sammy three times. Once
more he was chased by one of the small squirrels who was
resident in the wood and then he disappeared into the far end of
the quarry. He returned about four hours later in the same place
and this time in the company of the other squirrel. They seemed
to have come to a tolerant understanding and there was no sign
of aggression on this occasion at all.

Later in the evening, I turned on the watering spray for the
garden. It is one of those simple devices attached to a hose pipe,

which whizzes round under the force of the water. Sammy appeared and realised that this offered a new possibility of getting a drink. He endured the shower from the spray with a hesitant step and much shaking of whiskers and then walked to the centre of the equipment and tried to drink. He first got his nose stuck under the swinging arm, and in fact stopped it turning round till he'd had a good lick at the surplus water that was gathering round there. Then he removed his head and the sprinkler started shooting round again suddenly. The sudden swoosh that this caused produced instant alarm in the little squirrel, who shot off into the undergrowth and rattled up a tree as fast as his short legs would take him. Right at the very end of the evening I found Sammy collecting the birds' peanuts and storing them.

He seemed totally unafraid as I approached him, and in fact jumped up my jeans and ran round my legs before jumping off again. As he showed no sign of being at all cautious I felt sufficiently alarmed for him to move him along to the tree in which his box was placed. At the second attempt he finally stayed on the tree, and was persuaded to move higher and higher until he found his box and bedded in for the night. So, for a second day, Sammy had lived to enjoy his freedom.

The following morning I was up around seven-thirty and peered out through my bedroom window to see Sammy climbing the trees quite close by. So I quickly pulled my clothes on and trotted out into the cold air. I followed Sammy who wouldn't approach me, even though for the sake of my own curiosity I called him and tried to persuade him to come. He kept to the treetops and moved from one tree to another, doing half a circuit of the garden, until he shot up the horse chestnut tree in the far corner and disappeared over into the parkland and was subsequently seen in a tall beech tree.

That day, being Saturday, the family had arranged to visit my mother for the weekend and so by mid-morning we had left the house thinking Sammy safe at the top of a tree. We returned on Sunday to find a note tucked into my letterbox. It simply said 'John – Sorry, but we are very much afraid that a cat has killed Sammy. If you can bear to come and identify him he is in our garage. Eileen and Ron – number 4.'

11 A Death in the Family?

Not daring to tell my family, I hurried across to number 4 as my children prepared themselves for bed, quite oblivious to what might have happened to Sammy.

My neighbours' sad faces greeted me. I was taken to the separate brick garage nearby; we lifted the metal swing door and there, rolled in a sheet of newspaper, was a young squirrel that looked for all the world like Sammy. I tried to control my feelings and to assess objectively whether this really was my long-time friend. The corpse was quite limp, with its legs unnaturally extended fore and aft and showed no marks where it had been attacked. It certainly was a male and about Sammy's size, but the markings didn't quite seem to match Sammy; there was a grey patch that had started to develop at the base of his tail, and this corpse certainly had such a patch but it seemed bigger than I remembered. There were also grey patches developing on the flank as it was changing its coat. These too didn't seem to match precisely my memory of the patterning on Sammy. But I felt it was just wishful thinking.

It crossed my mind that earlier we had considered putting a

small mark on Sammy before we released him so that we could always identify him in the wild but we had decided against that on the insistence of the BBC film producer. Had we done so, it would have been useful now.

As I ran my eyes over the body, my mind jumped from one conclusion to the other. It really must be Sammy. Yet if it was, how come I wasn't a hundred per cent sure? The conclusion was inescapable. Perhaps the animal should never have been set free. After all, its mother was a cat to all intents and purposes. Now, the confidence in cats that we had given it had been betrayed.

The neighbours at number 4 filled me in on what had happened. The large black cat that lived next door was found by its owner on Saturday afternoon in their lounge with a squirrel lying by its side. The owner originally thought that the squirrel was not dead, because there were no marks upon it, so she rushed it down to my house only to find I was away. Not knowing this, she called for me, and in so doing attracted the attention of the neighbours at number 4. They were shocked at what had happened and offered to keep the body for me.

There was little I could do. I took the squirrel, thanked the neighbours, said that I wasn't really sure, but only ninety per cent certain that this was Sammy. I didn't want to give it more immediate attention that night because I didn't want to alarm my children, so I left it in my old potting shed with the garden tools. I put the boys to bed without telling them about my fears.

When I returned later to re-examine the corpse I found the newspaper empty. I realised to my horror that the rotten old door of the shed had enough space below it for a cat to have got in and stolen the by now slightly smelly corpse, so I no longer had the chance to inspect the animal's features in greater detail. Sammy as a baby was once scratched by one of the kittens and there used to be a minute mark in the middle of his forehead from the scratch where the hair had not grown uniformly. I'd hoped to look at this to see if I could locate that old sign to identify the animal as Sammy. But now this was not possible as the corpse was gone. I kicked myself for my own stupidity, but there was nothing I could do about it now.

I certainly felt that I had risked Sammy's life all for a film. You might say I could have kept him in a cage all his life, but it did seem to me that Sammy had a fair chance and releasing him was a risk worth taking. He'd certainly been saved, for if it had not been for me he would have died as a baby. He'd been brought up and I'd even seen him start to enjoy the freedom of living with the exuberance of a wild animal, bouncing around the fresh midsummer treetops. But that was now at an end.

I slept fitfully that night. Next morning I was tied up with various business meetings that meant that I was unable to go out to look for Sammy in my garden. However, later in the day I returned with Philip Sharpe, my assistant, and there, in one corner of the wood, was a small squirrel just the size of Sammy! Of course, it could be another squirrel. Possibly one of the two I had earlier released. I tried to approach it and it ran up the tree, and that made me think it was probably one of the others that I had seen around anyway. Sammy probably wouldn't have been as timid as that.

Next day in my garden we were watching again when a young squirrel visited the same place. It looked like the one we saw the previous day. It was slim and pale and it might have been Sammy although it wasn't possible to see whether it was a male or female. This time, it let us approach to within about twelve feet before shinning up a tree and running along my old quarry wall. Philip was thrilled at the sight for he felt totally confident that this animal was definitely Sammy. Philip had shared with me much of the daily responsibility of overseeing Sammy's development and so his conviction was a great relief to me. Whereas I still couldn't make my mind up, Philip definitely considered the markings matched Sammy's and he had seen him only a few days before. He also felt that the degree of confidence that the animal showed was greater than either of the other two young squirrels that he had hand-fed previously and we had released. In my heart, I confess that I was still by no means sure he was correct.

Our optimistic mood was increased that evening when a neighbour came to tell me that first thing in the morning a squirrel like Sammy had been seen sitting on the willow tree near my property and had allowed him to approach to within four feet. This suggested to him that it probably was Sammy, because none of the other squirrels nearby had ever come as close as that. Although I didn't see the occasion, the experiences of that day reintroduced in my heart a glimmer of hope that Sammy might still be alive.

The juvenile squirrel was seen many times over the next two months but it never again allowed us to get close to it. Furthermore, we could never be sure whether it was the same squirrel on each occasion. Twice we saw two juveniles together but that didn't help either because now, into midsummer, young squirrels in the wild were leaving their parents' nests and exploring new territories for themselves. If Sammy was still alive, he was just as likely to have gone off elsewhere on his own. Equally those could be new squirrels that were coming into my garden.

In an effort to solve the question of our squirrel's identity, I set our special squirrel traps which capture the animals without harming them. My aim was to check once again for the remains of the small scratch on Sammy's forehead. Over a two-week period, I caught two youngsters. One definitely wasn't Sammy on grounds of size, patterning and temper, while the other was a small male that did look like our old friend. He was relatively docile in the trap and was not apparently upset by our noses being pressed close to the wire. There was no sign of the small mark on the forehead, however, and when we opened the release door of the trap he chattered his teeth threateningly at us before bolting off and running up a tree. We were still none the wiser. Was this Sammy who had grown more wild after his period of liberation? Was this one of our hand-reared squirrels who was still living close by? Was Sammy still alive but had moved elsewhere? Or was Sammy dead?

12 Doubts and Uncertainties

For the next few months, we often saw young squirrels in the garden but, while fairly confiding, none of them would allow us to approach them closely. To keep up appearances for my children, I would often call out, 'Hey, come and look at Sammy!' when some timid youngster ventured fairly close to our home. But in my heart, I knew that Sammy would not have gone that wild that quickly. It was really a game I was playing with myself rather than admitting that we were never going to see our friend again.

In truth, I was becoming increasingly upset at my stupidity for risking Sammy's life in the wild. Not only was he especially vulnerable to cats of course, because of his upbringing but also he was released to join the ranks of wild squirrels in a country area where gamekeepers and foresters shoot them at every opportunity in an effort to keep their population down. Grey squirrels are alternately loved by the public in parklands and hated by many fair-minded country folk who consider them to be 'tree rats', villains in every way. I don't claim to know enough to judge whether their evil reputation is fully justified but I do have real doubts and uncertainties about how much trouble they really cause.

As I reflected on Sammy's possible fate, I found myself reviewing whether the habits of grey squirrels in Britain truly merited their bad image. The charge against them is based mainly on their feeding habits, their bark chewing and their effect on red squirrels. Taking each one in turn, there is another side to the argument which may not make us alter our views about grey squirrels but at least should be fairly considered. I felt it was sad if Sammy had been shot for something his species does not actually do.

The best known food of squirrels, of course, is nuts and in the autumn we watched and filmed as the squirrels in our garden collected acorns and beech nuts, and buried their spares. Typically as the winter proceeds, they still feed mainly on the nuts hidden from the previous autumn but in addition they will take young buds and some fungi as well as bulbs from our gardens. Later in the spring, they take more buds and shoots as well as the flowers including the catkins, of many trees.

It is at this time of the year that they are said to eat birds' eggs and nestlings which naturally makes them easy subjects for any-one wishing to taint them with unfavourable propaganda. However, as far as I know it has not been shown that squirrels affect the numbers of any wild bird population and I must confess that I feel their role in harming birds may have been greatly exaggerated.

I did try a simple experiment once to test this view using some fresh pheasant eggs provided by a helpful gamekeeper. Using the adult squirrels in the large enclosure at OSF, I made a simple 'scoop' similar to a pheasant's nest and put the clutch of eggs down for the animals to find. It was not long before one of our female grey squirrels found the eggs, sniffed at them cautiously and then moved off leaving them untouched. The same be-haviour was seen when the other squirrels encountered the eggs.

A female squirrel building
her nest inside a hollow
tree with oak leaves and grass

Above John Paling releasing Sammy
for the first time into the
wild *Right* Sammy's first foray
from his nest-box

An adult grey squirrel running
along the clothes–line in the
author's garden

An adult squirrel eating an acorn, the mainstay of its winter diet

Sammy – about an hour after his release – contemplating his new world

A squirrel chewing the bark of a sycamore tree

A squirrel sunning itself on a tree branch –
this is thought to produce vitamins in its
fur

Left and *Above* on opposite page:
Sammy's dramatic return on 20 January
1979

Right Sammy at home again: notice the
white distinguishing mark on the
squirrel's forehead

Overleaf Sammy – safe and sound
(copyright: Tony Evans)

They showed no sign of viewing them as food or trying to eat them.

This limited observation may not mean much on its own but my scepticism about the degree of damage caused by squirrels to bird populations was increased when I started to examine the pictorial evidence for egg-eating. In the first place, a senior scientist who studies squirrels recalls being on hand when propaganda 'still' photographs were taken of a squirrel eating a broken egg at the time when there was a vigorous government campaign to eradicate 'the tree rat'. These pictures were 'arranged' for the photographer and the egg in question was obligingly broken by a human! Also there exists a detailed documentary film of the private life of the red squirrel which has been transmitted on British and European television and this shows a squirrel raiding a bird's nest and eating an egg. However, if the sequence is analysed on a stopframe viewing machine it appears that the squirrel never eats the egg but is in fact feeding on food that has been smeared over the shell!

On the other hand, I do not doubt that wild squirrels do eat some bird eggs. Scientists at the famous Edward Grey Institute of Ornithology at Oxford have found undeniable evidence of squirrels chewing their way into wooden nest boxes and scoffing the eggs or young of the great tits and blue tits. Once they have chewed their way in, they don't appear to nest there which confirms the view that their raids on the bird boxes are for dietary rather than dormitory reasons. In addition local gamekeepers assure me they have seen squirrels stealing pheasant eggs and one reports that he has shot a squirrel with an egg still in its mouth. I accept the truth of both these stories, of course, but I simply wonder whether the grey squirrel does the amount of bird damage that is sometimes attributed to him.

If grey squirrels were really avid eaters of birds' eggs, I find it strange that many woodland birds survive. Grey squirrels have their well-established territories by the spring and they seem to know their area very thoroughly, and it is hard to believe that they would not be aware of most of the nests, particularly those in holes in trees in the area. Even if a mother bird were sitting on her nest, she would not be much of a match for a determined squirrel. Squirrels certainly oust starlings with ease.

I find it easier to believe that some grey squirrels do take eggs and nestlings during the spring but that they do not figure prominently on their diet. Stomach content analyses of wild squirrels also confirm this view.

Strangely perhaps, grey squirrels are subject to greatest food shortages in the period from May to July, a time when there appears to be the greatest variety of foods about. This is for two reasons: firstly the food that is around is of relatively poor nutrient value to squirrels and also it is then that the young squirrels from that year's births begin to enter the adult population to compete for the available food. In the battles for space that take place it is thought that the juniors tend to get pushed out from the better feeding areas to places such as young plantations where food for them appears to be in short supply. It is here of course that the squirrel's other much criticised behaviour – bark stripping – takes place. It is this, more than anything else, that makes foresters detest them.

Grey squirrels certainly do strip off the bark from young trees in midsummer and it seems obvious that this act will weaken if not kill growing trees. However, if you examine *why* they do it, it is just possible that by shooting them as they do, the gamekeepers may not be improving matters, and ironically may even be making matters worse.

There is a line of thought which reasons as follows. The best habitat for grey squirrels is mixed deciduous woodland as it provides not only an abundance of nuts in season but also many natural holes and hollows in the old trees. During the breeding season the pregnant females take over the best and most secure holes to build their breeding dreys and in doing this they will oust the males. So in the winter, when the gamekeepers go around pushing out the squirrels that live in the exposed dreys in the branches of trees, they are shooting mainly male squirrels at a time when they have already fulfilled their reproductive role and have mated with the females. The pregnant females are meanwhile occupying the most secure tree holes and will safely bring their litters to enter a world where there is less competition from adult males. Therefore many more of the youngsters may survive, the very ones thought to do the most damage!

Whatever the reason, there is no getting away from it, squirrels do eat bark at the height of the young trees' growing season and this causes considerable losses in plantations. However, putting aside the issues raised by shooting squirrels for sport (as they do on a massive scale in America) it seems possible that the cost of mounting squirrel shoots greatly exceeds the amount of extra damage that would have been caused if those animals had lived.

An answer which some foresters are resorting to is to stop planting extensive areas of sycamores and beech but instead to grow other tree species like ash, wild cherry and South American beech that are not attacked by the British grey squirrel.

The third and most emotional claim against the grey squirrel is that it has 'killed off' the red squirrels that used to thrive in Britain before the greys arrived. Again this simplification may be somewhat unfair. Firstly the greys neither eat the reds nor, in general, compete with them for their food. Part of the problem is that folklore has imbued the red squirrel with an image of shyness and gentleness and he is seen as the friend of mankind. Thus, red squirrels are painted as almost the 'little English gentleman' whereas the greys are cast as the hated foreign villains of the piece. This ignores the fact that before greys were introduced here, the red squirrel was admittedly more widespread but it was also guilty of bark chewing, just as the grey is now.

Another relevant fact is that the red never was a really well-adapted species in Britain. It is common on the continent of Europe (where greys have never survived despite several attempts to introduce them) but in Britain it is at the edge of its northern range. It has always been susceptible to diseases here and its population numbers fluctuated wildly even before the greys appeared.

It is known that the red squirrel population in Britain was actually diminishing due to natural disease at the time when the introduced greys were expanding in range. The red squirrel population would have gone down in numbers even if the greys had not been brought to our shores.

The reds survive best in extensive coniferous woodlands, areas that are less frequently to be found in overcrowded Britain. Only in Scotland and in areas like Thetford Chase in Norfolk is the species still surviving. Observers that have watched both species living side by side have found that there is virtually no sign of hostility between the two even at close range. If the species do compete, it is probably because the grey produces bigger litters and is more hardy and less fastidious as regards its habitat and food. On that basis, I would accept that the grey squirrel has been a major factor in accounting for the disappearance of the red squirrel from much of England. But the harsh image of the grey squirrel being a killer seems somewhat misplaced. After all, it was we who brought him here and now we have the problem of adjusting to the fact that the species is here to stay. It has been remarkably successful at breeding in the wild in Britain (though not in captivity!) and has become the countryman's enemy mainly because of its undoubted damage to trees. However I still think that a cool objective look needs to be given to the exact status of squirrels in Britain before we can be sure of the effectiveness of winter shoots.

But whatever the theories, there was no doubt that if Sammy had ever survived more than a day or two in the wild, he would be very vulnerable to the gun. Although his chances looked so pathetically slim in hindsight, we still had to have official permission to release him even though our squitten would make a totally insignificant addition to the grey squirrel population around Oxfordshire.

Despite the uncertainty of Sammy's whereabouts after the corpse was found, I kept peanuts available in my garden right through the summer when I knew there was likely to be a relative shortage of squirrel food. An assortment of squirrels of different sizes came at odd times to visit the garden but none of them looked like Sammy and none of them damaged any trees in my woodland.

As the winter approached it was comforting to see a young squirrel in the distance burying nuts under the fallen autumnal leaves. Once, when he was doing this, I saw a neighbour's cat stealthily hunt him. The squirrel was about eight feet from the trunk of a hefty horse chestnut and the large black cat froze as it first saw him. The cat lowered its body and slinked forward slowly, ears and eyes extended, alert for a pounce. As he approached to about ten feet away, the cat paused and the squirrel seemingly suddenly became aware of the danger and it shot back along the ground and up the tree, chattering its teeth noisily and shaking his stiff tail up and down. The cat cantered across to where the squirrel was as if to go half-heartedly through the motions and then totally ignoring the chattering squirrel, it walked away with a supercilious air as if to suggest it hadn't really been trying anyway! That squirrel for one was clearly aware that cats were to be avoided.

As winter hardened and the leaves had left the trees, one particular resident squirrel was seen to visit the bird table to steal the peanuts there. He would shin up the smooth metal tube and jump out and up to navigate the overhanging wooden table top. The birds became accustomed to this one adult consuming large quantities of their food and they would return to the table and sit feeding on the other end from the squirrel. He was still cautious of human observers however, and would leap off and run away over the lawns if I showed myself at the kitchen window.

With the onset of frosts and snow, the squirrel was joined by other squirrels who somehow had located a reliable supply of nuts in my garden feeders. One of them learnt to perform a hilarious tight-rope act across the washing on my clothes line in order to get to the top of the feeding table. He would start off from a tree and then flicking his tail to balance, he would hop along quickly. He would jump over the pegs and often miss his footing so he had to cling on grimly to, say, an item of underwear before he manoeuvred himself to the top of the line again. On the rare occasions he fell the ten feet or so to the ground, he never hurt himself and like a true trouper he usually returned to the start to try again.

Also the winter was the only time I have seen a squirrel drinking from the trees in the wild. One squirrel was exploring a sycamore branch early on a frosty morning as the sun was breaking through and melting that night's coating of frost. The squirrel turned to hang upside down on the branch and, with a spiral movement, went round licking off the water drops for two or three minutes non-stop. Once again, when I showed myself, the animal scurried away back along the branches and into the undergrowth of the old quarry wall. Increasingly it seemed that none of the squirrels in my garden showed anything of the tolerance for humans that I would have expected Sammy Squitten to have retained.

Another saddening fact was that none of the squirrels that visited my garden were using the wooden nest box that had been Sammy's home for so long. It remained high in the fork of a beech tree and was visited only by starlings and blue tits. During the autumn gales it blew down to the ground and I was able to examine the nest materials inside. It was very much as I had left it. All the nuts had gone but the soft vegetation was relatively undisturbed. There were no new leaves and no sign of a drey having been started.

We repaired the cracked box, put in more sacking, dried grass and a stock of peanuts and replaced Sammy's old home in the tree. Still it did not attract a resident. The local squirrels were obviously nesting elsewhere.

By the beginning of the new year, we had completed a year's filming on the project and all was complete except for the birth of the squirrel litter in the old oak tree. In fact we never did manage to persuade our own squirrels to mate and breed but we did obtain a litter of three orphaned babies and filmed them in a drey built by one of our adults in the hollow oak tree. These were the only pictures taken there so, in retrospect, our tree-moving exercise was an expensive waste of effort. Not for the first time, Nature had outwitted us.

Now the whole project was complete I was left with time to look back on the remarkable adventures of Sammy Squirrel with a better sense of perspective. Had I been wrong to risk the life of the infant squirrel by introducing it to a cat for a foster mother? Was it fair to breed and release a grey squirrel when people are still treating the species as vermin and are actively trying to keep their population down? Had I been kind or cruel to release an animal with such an unusual background into the wild? How objective could I be as a scientist when deciding the fate of an animal that was, if not a pet, at least a part of my family?

My conscience is still clear on the topic of fostering Sammy on a cat. His only chance of survival was to be taken over totally by some mother substitute. If it hadn't been Beauty, the cat, it would have been me and pipettes of cow's milk! In either event he was to be brought up by an abnormal foster parent with the consequent problem that his subsequent behaviour to other squirrels would be awry. In the circumstances, providing a careful watch was kept on the cat during two crucial phases (when the baby squirrel was first introduced and when it first started to run in an un-kittenlike manner), the squirrel stood a much better chance of survival being mothered by the cat. What's more the experience did reveal just how deeply ingrained and unalterable were the first basics of squirrel behaviour in Sammy, and kitten behaviour in Pickles, Charlie and Scruf. We ourselves had learnt a lot at a superficial level and might even have sparked off some biochemical research project to account for why it is that cat's milk is so suitable for squirrels. One never knows at the time what full significance can be drawn from observations on unusual animal interrelationships.

Naturally, like a parent, I wanted the best for my foster child and I had always hoped he might be returned to the freedom of the wild. I had obviously been concerned that he might not have been suited to life in the woods but I had tried to assess how well he would fare before releasing him. He knew well how to look after himself in the rough and tumble of life with a family of kittens. He knew no fear in dealing with adult squirrels. He ran away from a dog and the smell of a strange cat. From his earliest days he always had shown a schizophrenic urge to flee from the cats and me whenever he was allowed outside in the garden. Towards the end, he was fed in such a way that he would not associate humans with food and so in all these ways we had done about as much as we could to test how he would survive if he were to be released.

Yet despite all this, Sammy had disappeared and a cat had killed a young squirrel. As time passed I was left with a dull feeling that my worst fears must be true. Certainly, I would advise anyone against bringing up a squirrel in captivity and then finally releasing it into the wild. The most likely result would be a speedy death.

13 The Happy Wanderer

On the morning of 20 January, a fairy tale came true. It had been snowing hard the day before and the family's planned visit to relatives up north had been called off at the last minute as a result of an early morning 'phone call reporting heavy falls and dangerous roads. Adjusting to the change of plans, I went into the kitchen to prepare a leisurely breakfast and I looked out across the lawns to the wood to see how bad the weather was locally. There had been something of a thaw for the paths were partly visible below the slush but the scene was bleak and wintry.

As I looked, a perky light grey head appeared over the brow of the lawn and a young squirrel approached the bird feeder. He had white tips to his ears and was sufficiently small to be clearly one of the past year's generation. As a photographer, I mentally cursed the fact that animals only ever seem to show confidence and to come close on occasions when one doesn't have a camera to hand!

He stopped about ten feet from the kitchen window and snuffled around looking for food so I crept into the lobby, took a handful of the peanuts I keep for the birds and gingerly opened the door to throw them out. The squirrel stood on its hind legs eyeing me alertly – but it didn't run off. I gently lobbed the peanuts into the snow near its feet and it held its ground for a moment before picking up a nut in its front feet and sitting down to eat it.

The fact that it didn't dash away when the nuts landed close to it struck me immediately as unusual but I felt vaguely that it may be desperate for food because of the hard winter and this had made it so bold. But as the cold of the outdoors hit my morning face, I suddenly became aware of an uncanny familiarity about the expression and shape of its head. I was looking at Sammy! He was distinctly different from all the other young squirrels I had been seeing around.

Tense with elation, I sneaked back indoors and ran through the house calling out my discovery to my sons. I raced out of the front door across the drive in my slippers and collected my tripod and movie camera from the garage. In very little time I was back indoors, trying to avoid panicking at the conflict between wanting to keep an eye on the squirrel and wishing to set up all my filming equipment.

Mark and Sean were in the kitchen by now but they reported that the squirrel had run off almost as soon as I had called them. He had disappeared out of sight down one side of the house.

Our discovery was so wonderful, yet still almost unbelievable to me that I desperately wanted to record it on film so I set up the camera looking out towards the bird table in the hope that Sammy would return. Before all was ready, Sean came bounding into the kitchen, wide-eyed and urgent. Sammy was trying to get into the lounge through the closed French window!

We all charged through the house at a gallop and then pulled up to a snail's pace as we peeped into the lounge. Sure enough, there was Sammy running along the outside of the long French window, repeatedly standing on his back legs and pattering his front feet on the dirty, splashed glass as he looked in. There was no mistaking his intention; possibly he had seen something he recognised which had excited him. I dashed back for my camera, telling the boys to keep their distance until I returned.

Thirty seconds later I was back with peanuts and camera. He was still there. Slowly, I moved to the window with an intense sense of excitement, yet with total confidence knowing, somehow in advance, what was going to happen. Sammy came directly towards me and, as I crouched, he scrabbled up with his front feet against the glass that separated us. As that appeared to offer no way in, he dropped down and once more ran up and down along the outside of the ground-level window. I unlocked the door, banged the winter-jammed wood from its frame and swung it open.

Without hesitation Sammy came in, body held low, and sniffed my outstretched hand. He ran past me, sniffed the coffee table and ran outdoors again, but he only went about five yards away before briskly returning a few seconds later.

The whole happening seemed unreal, like a dream. I was so overjoyed at this reunion that it seemed to be taking place at high speed before my senses could properly take it all in. All sorts of thoughts and emotions were racing through my mind. Relief was the overriding sensation coupled with simple delight at seeing him back fit and well. It occurred to me, even then, that I must have been so shocked after the cat had killed the young squirrel that I must have been fooling myself trying to believe that other squirrels in my garden were in fact Sammy.

Breaking all my rules, I offered our visitor a peanut and he confidently put one paw on my hand as he took it from my fingers. Not stopping to eat it, Sammy carried the nut in his mouth as he explored more of the room before dashing out-doors again. This time he went some fifty feet away across two lawns and over the garden. I lost sight of him but the boys had a better vantage point and very soon reported, 'He's coming back.' Sure enough Sammy ran full speed over the snow, across the path and inside the lounge again.

He allowed me to stroke him before rushing off on top of the coffee table leaving muddy paw marks reminiscent of bygone days. Then he did a round of the easy chairs and cushions – a favourite old playground – before pattering across the carpet again and taking another peanut from my hand as I sat on the floor by the open door. By now we had had plenty of time to study the condition of our old pal.

First there was no doubt in any way that this was our original Sammy. Not only was his behaviour towards us and his familiarity with the house so amazing but also he still had the small distortion of the fur on his forehead from one of his step-kittens' claws. It wasn't really necessary to confirm his identity with a check of his sex but at Mark's insistence, we did look and saw that our visitor was indeed a male.

To our eyes, Sammy was in splendid condition. He was smaller and more slightly built than I would have imagined him to be. He had shorter claws in proportion to his feet since we had last seen him and his tail was more handsome and bushy. There was a second small mark, a new one, on the top of his nose which could easily have resulted from fighting with another squirrel. After all, it was over six months since we had last definitely set eyes on Sammy and no doubt he had had many encounters with friends and foes during that time. He clearly had plenty of energy now as he rushed out and away to the base of the quarry wall to bury his nut before scampering back to us once more.

Although I couldn't analyse it in words, his face had exactly the same 'mood' and alert expression as our Sammy of old. His new white wisps to his ears gave him a slightly different look on first sight which seemed rather as if he had a new brushed back hair style. He was also fatter than when we let him go. When he sat on his haunches munching food, he looked round and chubby but this changed to his sleek lithe look as he ran around the house followed by my two entranced boys.

It was just like old times. He soon found the fruit bowl and ran off with an enormous apple which he chewed messily on the arm of a chair. He next tried to bury food in all the old nooks and crannies around the building. One peanut was placed literally in each corner of the dining-room while others were tapped into place in the cushions, between the logs and deep into the (cold) ash below the fire grate, an incident which resulted in much sneezing and clouds of white ash which he wiped off all over the furniture.

Back in the kitchen he showed that he could now easily leap directly from the floor to the worktop surfaces in one bound. He pattered along, knocking my cookery books over, scattering soil from the plant pots, slipping on some papers, drinking some detergent-loaded water in which some towels were soaking, providing a liberal sprinkling of droppings before jumping into the boys' large model-making kit and scattering the tiny plastic components across the floor. Sammy was back!